MORE
SMALL WATER
TROUT FISHING
IN THE SOUTH

Other books by Graeme Pullen

Fishing in the Isles of Scilly
A Guide to Small Water Trout Fishing in the South
The Alternative Holiday Guide to Deep Sea Fishing around Europe
The Graeme Pullen Guide to Freshwater Fishing Baits
The Graeme Pullen Guide to Sea Fishing Baits
Big Game Fishing – The Great Adventure
Go Fishing for Shark
Go Fishing for Cod
Go Fishing for Trout
Go Fishing for Tench
Go Fishing for Bass
Go Fishing for Chub and Barbel
Go Fishing for Pike
Go Fishing for Carp

MORE

SMALL WATER TROUT FISHING

IN THE SOUTH

GRAEME PULLEN

ASHFORD
Southampton

Published in 1990 by Ashford, Buchan & Enright Ltd,
  1 Church Road
  Shedfield
  Hampshire
  SO3 2HW

While great care has been taken in the compilation of this book, the author and publisher cannot guarantee that all the details, such as prices, schedules, addresses and telephone numbers will remain unchanged and exactly as quoted here. The author has no connection with any business or establishment listed here, and no guarantee or endorsement is implied or given in this respect. That a business or establishment is not listed or detailed does not imply any criticism. The impressions and opinions expressed in this book are subjective and readers must make their own judgements on everything presented here.

The author would like to thank all the fishery owners who assisted him with factual information for this book.

British Library Cataloguing in Publication Data

Pullen, Graeme
  More small water trout fishing in the south.
  1. Southern England. Angling waters: Trout fisheries
  I. Title
  799.1'755

  ISBN 1–85253–215–7

Typeset by Acorn Bookwork, Salisbury, Wiltshire
Printed by Hartnolls Limited, Bodmin, Cornwall, England

Cover photograph: Graeme Pullen

Contents

Location map	vi
Introduction	1
How do trout get there?	2
Choosing tackle	7
Avon Springs	11
Chiphall Lake	21
Church Hill Farm	29
Dorset Springs Lakes	37
Halliford Mere	45
Hazel Copse	55
Horton	65
John O'Gaunt's Lakes	75
Ladywell Lakes	81
Mopley Farm	89
Nythe Lakes	97
Powder Mills and Weston	105
Robinswood	115
Rooksbury Mill	123
Wattlehurst	133
Whitesheet	139

SELECTED TROUT FISHERIES IN THE SOUTH OF ENGLAND

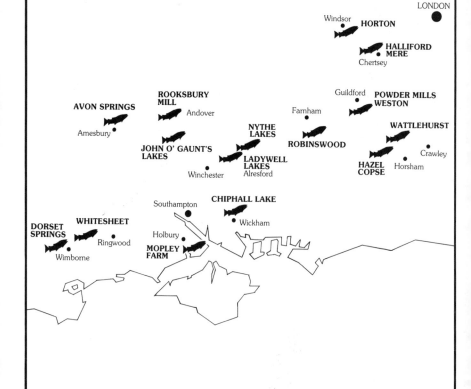

● Milton Keynes

CHURCH HILL FARM
Mursley

● Aylesbury

LONDON ●

Windsor **HORTON**

HALLIFORD MERE
Chertsey

ROOKSBURY MILL
Andover

Guildford **POWDER MILLS WESTON**

AVON SPRINGS
Amesbury

Farnham

WATTLEHURST

NYTHE LAKES

ROBINSWOOD

JOHN O' GAUNT'S LAKES

LADYWELL LAKES
Winchester   Alresford

HAZEL COPSE   Horsham

Crawley

CHIPHALL LAKE

Southampton

Wickham

DORSET SPRINGS   **WHITESHEET**
Holbury
Ringwood

MOPLEY FARM
Wimborne

INTRODUCTION

Like its highly successful predecessor, *A Guide to Small Water Trout Fishing in the South*, this is a guide the fly fisherman can pick up at any time in order to choose a venue of which he may have had no previous experience. Lord knows it's infuriating to fish new waters for an entire day with a black fly, only to learn on your return to the lodge that everything always comes out on a white fly! I make no attempt at beguiling the reader with the complexities of higher entomology. I feel that, like me, you will want a fish or two on your line and in a reasonably short time. You may also be relieved to learn that I have no personal vested interest in any fishery. The venues I have included are all waters I have visited myself, so you will get in each case an unbiased appraisal from an ordinary trout angler like yourself.

The small water trout fisheries are here to stay and provide thousands of fishermen with the chance to catch a good-sized rainbow or brown in conditions that are often sheltered, with clear water, and where there is a stocking density that at least assures you of as much success as the next man. You will not find this book littered with pictures of jumbos all caught by the same person. I visit when the average angler fishes. I hear his moans, his groans, his opinions, and his delights, so I am in an excellent position to write as balanced an account of each water as you are ever likely to get. Many fishery owners will appreciate this, as it is you, the travelling angler, that they most wish to visit their waters.

I am sure you will find this second collection of trout fisheries in the south every bit as rewarding as the first.

HOW DO TROUT GET THERE?

Almost every angler has some idea of how trout grow, and there are many reliable books on the intricacies of the subject. Modern methods of research into the various diseases and their causes and treatment made the art of trout farming a more secure occupation. It may interest a few of the newcomers to learn about its basics, and in this way they will appreciate fully that the trout they catch are hand-fed, and not wild.

There has always raged a controversy over the merits of wild as opposed to artificially reared trout. As the pressure on flyfishing has increased, so the demand for value-for-money wild trout fisheries has become impractical. A hundred years ago trout fishing was undertaken mainly in flowing water, and the primary species was the brown trout. Then along came the fast-growing rainbow with its acrobatics on being hooked, its culinary virtues, and its freedom in taking the fisherman's fly. In addition, the rainbow was a faster grower than the brown, and therefore soon took over. While a truly wild fish is one that has been laid as an egg by another wild fish, and grows to a good size under normal conditions, the rainbow presents a complete contrast. Rarely do rainbow trout breed in the wild, and what is now thought of as a 'wild' fish is one introduced into a large reservoir as a fingerling, and which, fending for itself, grows to a respectable size.

While the small stillwater fisheries stock with fish bigger on average than those in reservoirs, a fish from the latter is a whole different ball game when hooked. A reservoir rainbow leaps more, has more stamina, has no damaged fins, and displays a full silver body that defies description. As a fingerling it will still have been reared artificially, but it is 'free range', as opposed to 'battery'. All the small stillwater farms do is to feed the fish longer. To get a proper insight into this, I interviewed the manager of Avington Fisheries, Roy Ward.

Few would dispute the fast growth rate of the Avington rainbow, and they have taken the British record for a variety of trout species over the years. First you need pure, clean spring water. Although the stock ponds at Avington are fed by the river Itchen, the egg and fry hatchery is fed only by pure bore-hole water, so that it is as clean as possible. As a basis for a good egg, you need a good stock to breed from. Roy looks after his brood fish to ensure that when he strips the eggs, only the best are produced. He has refined a fast-growing strain of trout, so why should he let it deteriorate? Roy strips the fish throughout November, and although some text books state that 700 eggs come from each pound of body weight, he thinks that it may go as high as 2000 for an 8 lb rainbow. He runs a batch of brood fish in the 7–10 lb range. You can usually reckon on stripping milt from one male and mixing it with the eggs of three females, but Roy sometimes uses a one-to-one mixture.

After fertilization, the eggs are placed in incubator jars, each holding about five gallons of water, and mounted some 2 ft from the floor. This method allows Roy to use the minimum area for the maximum eggs, whereas some trout farms use up a lot of floor space by placing them in trays. The water from the bore hole is run through a 'header' tank by gravity feed, to oxygenate the water as much as

Avington's fishery manager Roy Ward runs his bore-hole water straight through these large glass jars. Inside are thousands of trout eggs, the pure, highly oxygenated water maximizing the hatch rate of eggs. The water runs through the eggs, then spills over the edge of the jars.

3

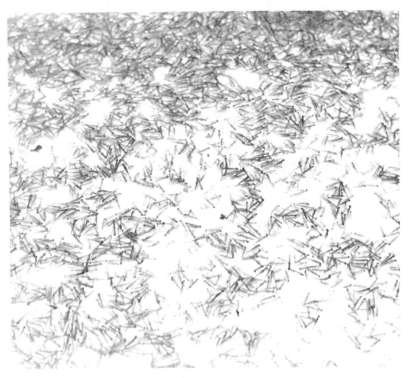

Once hatched, the fry are moved to darkened shallow troughs, with highly oxygenated water running through to ensure healthy fish. At this stage they are fed with a powdered food with a high protein content.

possible before it runs through the incubator jars. Roy can hold 100,000 eggs in each jar, the water pressure gently vibrating the eggs for a slight movement. Mortality during this critical egg stage is understandably high, but from the egg stage to saleable fish Roy reckons he has a 60 per cent success rate.

The eggs hatch in 26 days and are then placed in concrete raceways, where natural spring water is run through the shallow troughs. The hatching eggs are suspended in fine metal trays, which allow the hatching fry to drop through, leaving the dead eggs and underdeveloped fry in the tray for easy removal. They stay in these concrete raceways for three to four weeks, feeding only on the remains of their eggs sacks. After this stage they start to take the first of the high-protein feed, which comes first as a fine powder and is later given as graded grains of feed. (Avington gets through a staggering 15 tons of high-protein trout feed each season.) The Fry

When they have reached several inches, the fry are taken from the hatchery troughs and placed outside in the open stews. Roy Ward feeds the stock ponds several times a day, their surface boiling as thousands of fish race to grab the pellets. From here they are graded to separate the fast growers from standard stock. The next item of food they see should be the angler's fly, when they have been stocked into the lakes.

are kept in the raceways until they weigh approximately one hundred fish to the pound, at which time it is safe enough to take them out into the river water, the bore-hole water being almost free of diseases and bacteria. There are many different diseases, but as the fry continue to grow, they develop their own system of natural defence.

The following November, exactly one year after the egg was mixed with the milt, the fish will be about 9 in in length, but fish farms supplying the table trade will push their fish even larger by intensive feeding. For the stocking of another water most fisheries now require a 2 lb fish, which would be around two years old. After three years of feeding, Roy has a 7–10 lb fish, while a four year old may be 9–15 lb, and a five year old 20 lb. Roy explained that, just like humans and animals, some fish turn out to be faster growers than others. He thinks they could go on just over five years, while others think rainbows could live longer than eight years. As a guide, wild browns in a natural feeding environment may grow to even ten or twelve years old.

As well as pushing around 12,000 2 lb–plus rainbows through his farming facility, Roy has seen all the hybrids: the tiger trout, which was a brook brown cross; the cheetah, which is a brook rainbow cross; and the brookie itself, which is a species in its own right, and related to the char. He can deliver his stock anywhere by pumping a water tank full of highly oxygenated water, using commercial oxygen bottles. It is even possible to transport fish internationally by aircraft. In Canada and the United States trout are 'seeded' into an inaccessible water by dropping them from a low-flying aircraft as it skims the surface.

There you have a glimpse of how a fish farm produces the trout you catch from a small stillwater. Fish farms supply both the food trade and the requirements of fishermen. Whether you agree with intensive feeding or not, the small waters are here to fill a void, and if there were no such farms, then you would have few trout to catch.

CHOOSING TACKLE

The selection and use of fly fishing tackle can always be left to the individual. Assuming you have a basic grasp of what a fly rod, reel, and line look like, and understand the principles that make them work, you should address your attention to the actual fishing. Too many people seem to get caught up with 'posing' with all the 'right' tackle, partly because the sport of trout fishing is traditionally fashionable. As for the flies themselves, fishermen all over the world are constantly on the prowl for the magic pattern that will have trout falling over themselves to grab it. By contrast, I was never one to follow fashions; nor did I swagger round the fisheries with all the lastest super equipment. My concern has always been to sink a hook into a trout's jaw, and to that end I have been fairly successful.

Once you have tried other aspects of the sport, it is easy to drop into flyfishing. I have no hesitation in stating that one of the most incredibly stupid and gullible fish is the trout. It is so easy to catch by normal methods that it had to be protected by restricting tactics to casting a fly. If you care to run a freelined lobworm down the River Itchen or put a Mepps spinner in one of the River Test pools you would see how gullible trout can be. You would also be hung, drawn, and quartered, so I mention this purely tongue in cheek.

Flycasting is in itself a pleasurable way of casting, but what about the properties of a fly rod for applying pressure to a fish? Or that tiny reel, invariably without a drag system save for the clicker mechanism? I think the time has come for manufacturers to launch into some new centre drag fly reels, or rods with an extendable butt to allow the rod blank to be flexed along the forearm. But then these are my ideas, and after you have spent a few years 'under the rod' yourself, you too may feel there is room for a change. The basic fly rod for any of the stillwaters described in this book should be of carbon fibre, or a carbon/fibreglass mix, and about 9ft long. There is little need for ultra-long casts, and to that end the line weight should be a little over that of the rod's capabilities. An overrated line-to-rod ratio will ensure you fire out the casts better, and should that line be of the weight-forward variety, then your mistakes will be ironed out by the carrying capacity of the line.

You need just three types of line. I have been using Airflo lines for a while now and they seem to have the edge in quality. For dry fly and nymph fishing you will need a floating line. There are intermediates and slow sinks but if you are a complete newcomer to flyfishing, the last thing you want is to be baffled by the range of different line weights available. To the floating line you attach your nylon leader, which should be around 9 ft long, but perhaps as long as 12 ft on hot, still summer days. This can be degreased with a sinking paste which allows you to retrieve a nymph or small lure just beneath the surface. Or you can grease it with a mucilin leader floatant which ensures your dry fly will stay on top of the surface film. So with the one floating line you have two options to try.

I would then advise going to a medium-sink line, which for most of the depths you are likely to encounter in the fisheries listed, is quite sufficient. You can fish a medium-sink as deep as you want simply by waiting longer for the line to drop through the depths. My advice is to try a retrieve after, say, ten seconds, then twenty, then thirty, trying to remember the number when you hit a fish. This is called the countdown technique and is ideal for a thorough search of the depths.

If you are fishing a deep pool or hole, knowing full well that the fish are down deep, then use a fast-sink line. This heavier line is better suited to late-autumn and winter fishing, when the water temperatures will have pushed the trout deeper and made them more lethargic. Your best bet with a fast-sink line is to grease the leader, and use a buoyant pattern of fly such as a muddler. This stops the hook picking up leaves, twigs, and other rubbish deposited on the lake bed during the gales of late autumn, and fishes the fly well inside the trout's 'kill' zone. This technique of using a greased leader and a sunk line allows you to fish very slowly with your retrieve, which is very useful since the trout takes will be more gentle in colder weather.

You can choose any fly reel, as in my opinion they are all merely line-storage devices. Until someone comes up with a geared, centre-drag fly reel my view will remain unchanged. You need two fly boxes. A wallet with a styrofoam insert is ideal for nymphs and lures. With dry flies you need to ensure that they are loose and that the hackles are not crushed. Treat yourself to one of those multi-partitioned fly boxes with hinged lids. Watch out for windy weather when you open it, as a gust of wind can deposit all your best dry flies over half the country-side, where they will blend in superbly! You need a good landing net, preferably a 20-inch model with a telescopic or extending handle. You need a priest to whack the trout over the head. Don't waste good money on a shop-bought priest – a small piece of copper tube with some lead packed in one end does the same job.

Flyfishing jackets are great on summer days, when you can wander around with the bare minimum of gear. But how many fine days do we get? By all means get one, but choose a heavier coat like a Barbour to cope with all weather conditions. You'll need a good hat with a broad peak to shut down the sunlight. I use a professional guide's hat with sunflaps for the ears and neck. You can buy them in the USA, and quite why nobody has started importing them into the UK yet is beyond me. You need a pair of good polarizing glasses – not just to cut down the glare, but to cut down the risk of planting your fly in your eyeball. I saw a photo once of an angler with a fly lodged about $\frac{1}{8}$ in in his eye, right past the barb, and a whisker from his pupil! I never forgot that picture and fish in glasses even in the rain! The best tint to get is brown, though the grey glasses are good. You will also, I hope, require a wicker bag to carry your fish around. If it is high summer, gut them at the fishing hut as soon as possible and place them in a cool box, as they can go off in a few hours of freak summer sunshine. The ASW Coolfishbag is custom-made for keeping fish chilled, and can also be used for the angler's own food.

Finally, start to take an interest in fly tying as early as you can. It serves to expand your knowledge of exactly what a fly does under water, enables you to make up your patterns and of course you save an enormous amount of money on shop flies. Buy a few to copy, then make your own flies. Good hunting!

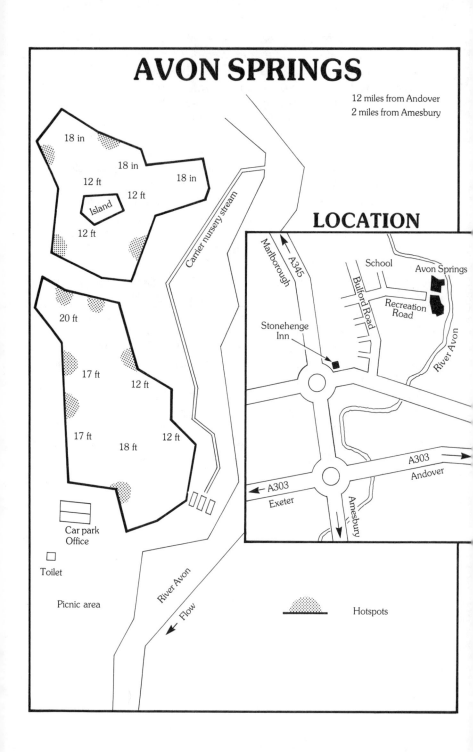

AVON SPRINGS

12 miles from Andover
2 miles from Amesbury

18 in

18 in

18 in

12 ft

12 ft

Island

12 ft

Carrier nursery stream

20 ft

17 ft

12 ft

17 ft

12 ft

18 ft

Car park
Office

Toilet

Picnic area

River Avon

Flow

LOCATION

Marlborough

A345

School

Avon Springs

Bulford Road

Recreation
Road

River Avon

Stonehenge
Inn

A303

Andover

A303

Exeter

Amesbury

Hotspots

AVON SPRINGS

A new water offering Wiltshire anglers yet another quality venue is Avon Springs, at Durrington. Many small trout fisheries are run by people who were previously either anglers or involved in trout farming in some way, but this fishery has been built from nothing by a man who until recently had never fished for trout. Owner Barrie Bawden has been in the motor trade in nearby Amesbury for over 40 years. Now he has taken a step into semi-retirement, leaving his son and son-in-law holding the fort as far as business goes. Barrie's first outing to a fishery was to Andover's Dever Springs, and once he had felt the thrill of a trout tearing line from his fingers, he was 'hooked'. It was by pure coincidence that he heard about the land coming up for sale from which the fishery is now constructed. A phone call from the owner of the land, who was a good friend of his father, prompted Barry to put his solicitors in touch with the landowner. He soon became the owner of several hundred yards of the prime Wiltshire Avon chalk stream. Incidentally, he informed me that not one stretch of this famous river is in public ownership, all of its fish-filled length being privately owned.

Suggestions followed from friends and the Wessex Water Authority that Barrie's land was tailor-made for the construction of a trout fishery. He soon got in touch with adjoining landowners and, since there were no objections, set about digging out the two lakes and stew pond that now form the fishery. The site was formerly a wetland, and Barrie had all the relevant soil analyses done, including having the Wessex Peat Company analyse the peat for acidity. The sample came back with a report that said it had a neutral pH value of 6.5 and was over 5000 years old. The site where the office now stands was excavated to a depth of 18 ft, and solid-oak sluices were discovered, indicating that the river's former route was totally different from what it is today.

The property was roughly rectangular, with a small nursery stream running into and around a three-acre plot, creating an island. This stream was fed by a natural spring, bubbling up from a tiny pond, gin-clear and pure. The land was completely waterlogged and un-usable, so the first problem during the excavation was how to keep the ground dry so that the digger could work unhindered. The top, smaller, lake was the first to be excavated. But immediately the digger became waterlogged as springs were broken into, releasing water at an alarming rate. The lake filled up with water almost as fast as it could be pumped out. There formed a small island in the centre, which is still there, because the water filled in so quickly that the digger could not excavate it. When this two-acre water was finished, the main lake of five acres was begun.

Aware of the problems of excess water, Barrie obtained a pump that extracted it at a rate of 91,000 gallons per hour. The first lake had filled up within 48 hours, so the use of a pump for the larger lake was of paramount importance. The pump was used non-stop for just under a year, except for oil changes. A carrier stream that ran around the outside of the boundary was also dredged, to form an obstacle to unwanted visitors. A lake full of trout with no resident on site meant something had to be done about security, so a gate and fencing also followed. The larger lake is very deep – 18 ft in places – and about 35,000 tons of gravel were removed.

All that remained now was the construction of some stews in which Barrie could hold a stock of fish for topping up the lakes. This was easily done, the nursery stream from the main spring being used to feed the stews, thus preventing water from the lake creating any spread of disease. With the small lake at the top of the property dropping to 12 ft, and the large lake to 18 ft, clearly some stock had to be put in. In September 1987 around 350 rainbow trout were placed into the small lake to take their chance while everything was tidied up. They weighed around 14 oz each and were fed regularly through the entire winter of 1987–8. The following May they were found to weigh nearly 3 lb each, and boasted silver flanks and full tails. Of this initial stock 195 fish were put into the large lake and 43 into one of the stews. The latter batch contained the faster growers, and with intensive feeding it is hoped these will provide the nucleus of a population of really large rainbows for both lakes.

Barrie buys in other small rainbows and feeds them on to around 3 lb as the mainstay of daily stocking. Even though the lakes were finished only in June 1988, and opened in August of the same year, the venue has already achieved some creditable statistics. Andover regular Joan Rogers used a Christmas Tree lure and 6 lb leader to take a limit bag of trout weighing 3 lb 6 oz, 4 lb, 5½ lb and 6 lb. Even

Andover angler Joan Rogers displays a fine 7½ lb Avon Springs rainbow which was taken on a Christmas Tree lure, fished on a sinking line close to the bank.

The owner of Avon Springs, Mr Barrie Bawden, casts a line for grayling in his section of the Hampshire Avon. This pool was said by Frank Sawyer to be the best grayling pool on the Avon.

as I wrote this, Barrie telephoned to tell me that Joan's record rainbow of 7½ lb had just been beaten by a 9½ pounder! By the time this book becomes available, I imagine that the record will be near 13 or even 15 lb.

This part of the Wiltshire countryside is only 3 miles from Stonehenge and Salisbury is only half an hour's drive away, so the fishery is ideal for the family man. While his wife and children either picnic or tour the historic area, he can fish. Alternatively, there are enough shops in Salisbury to keep any woman happy! In the future, the acquisition of more land adjacent to the fishery will allow Barrie to put other plans into operation. He hopes to landscape the area further and construct a restaurant and bar with full facilities, and given the speed with which he has built the fishery, I think that it will happen soon.

With Barrie's ownership now extended to over 1350 yards of the Wiltshire Avon, there should also be the chance to try some of the best grayling and brown trout fishing on this excellent river. While I was there I saw dozens of grayling to around 1 lb, and the largest caught there to date weighed 2 lb 10 oz. In fact the Wessex Water Authority removed some 30,000 grayling from this area of the river, and found it was one of the few places where they breed prolifically. The river here has not been fished from Barrie's bank for some 50 years, apart perhaps by the local poacher, so it is difficult to give advice on the beats or stretches that fish the best. It is far better to ask Barrie when you phone up – he will be delighted to give you what information he can.

At present the small, clear top lake is available to the dry-fly enthusiast. The fly life, because the lakes are so close to the river, is amazing. I saw one angler take a limit of four fish from this lake, off the top, in November!

APPROACH AND TACKLE

As for tackle, only conventional fly-fishing equipment is allowed. Tandem lures, double or treble hooks, spinners and baits are prohibited. No hooks larger than size 10 are allowed, and the dressed length of the fly should not exceed 1 in. Wading is prohibited on both of the lakes. Continuing to fish after a limit bag of fish has been taken is not allowed, nor is the sharing of a bag limit or of a rod. Landing nets must always be carried. No leader of less than 6 lb may be used, and all fish caught must be killed. No litter or discarded fishing line

One in the landing net for 'Pop' Rogers, a regular at Avon Springs. This fish fell to a Christmas Tree lure fished slowly near the bottom.

must be left, and dogs, radios and other possible sources of nuisance are not allowed. Starting time is 8.30 AM and fishing ends half an hour after sunset. These rules are basically the same as for any other well-run water.

SEASONAL TACTICS

Spring

The depth of both lakes causes the water temperature to remain constant for some time. If it has been a bad winter, the cold water will be slow to warm, and therefore a slower retrieve at a greater depth than normal would be required. A fast-sink Airflo line or similar, but with the leader greased, and with an orange lure such as a Whisky Fly, should pick up the fish. If the winter has been unseasonally mild, the water will gain temperature a little more quickly. There is no need for outsize lures – stick to the 1-in requirement, and ensure that the Marabou is tied to within that length. Best patterns are: Ace of Spades, Zulu, Christmas Tree, and Appetiser.

Summer

This venue lends itself perfectly to dry-fly fishing, and although the smaller lake is in any case restricted to this method, I have seen a lot of sport enjoyed on the large lake by surface fishermen. Buzzers fished slowly in the surface film, preferably across a ripple, will score heavily, especially on warm evenings. Stalking the margin drop-off by the deep water where the two lakes join will bring better-quality fish to anyone using a leaded nymph. Patterns to try are Mayfly, Green Beast, Montana, and the like. Most of these small waters respond to much the same patterns. The mayfly is so prolific, owing to the proximity of the Avon, that you would be missing good sport if you neglected to imitate it. Try casting into any breeze from the car-park end of the main lake. Most anglers use a floating line for their nymph work, but I am a great believer in slow-sink lines because they allow you to get a laterally deeper retrieve. Airflo produce an enormous range. Try the dry flies and sedges on the small lake in the early morning, moving to the larger lake when any ripple starts to appear. As this lake is nearest the spring, water clarity should be excellent and you should be able to cast to individual fish.

Autumn

Stay with the weighted nymph patterns of Mayfly and Montana during August and September. The springs feeding the lakes will ensure a constant temperature, so insect life will still be prolific. Do a lot of margin walking on the larger lake. There is a definite drop-off here, and I noticed a lot of bigger fish in the 4 lb-plus range moving about. The long caster will pick up fish in the large lake by using very small lures and a sinking line with a small, jerky retrieve. Watch out for last-minute crash-takes.

Winter

The last time I fished here there were trout rising in the middle of November. I was in fact checking out the superb grayling fishing on the river and almost wanted to backcast into the trout lakes! No need to stay with nymphs now − just try a few casts with them in the surface layers, then bring your fly back deeper, much faster than you would normally. Often this evokes a response from trout that have been in the water any length of time. The larger lures − and Barrie Bawden would be the best person to advise you on effective patterns − will score heavily if fished deep and fast. Since this is a brand-new water there should be no coarse fish fry, so the trout will be moving about a lot, rather than bottling up in a small area.

GENERAL INFORMATION

The standard facilities of car park, WC, picnic area and ticket office are in operation at present, but hopefully the new restaurant and bar complex will be open soon. A tackle shop with all the requirements and fly patterns is also part of this planned development.

Avon Springs is destined to become a regular fishing venue for the small water enthusiast, and with the proposed new refreshment facilities, it should prove to be a great place to fish. The fishery is open all the year round. The entire venue can be privately booked for parties of more than sixteen. Advance booking is advisable since word of a top-quality water soon gets around on the trout-fishing grapevine.

Ticket prices for 1990 are as follows:

Day ticket (full day): £22.00 (four-fish limit).
Half-day ticket (to or from 2 PM): £18.00 (three-fish limit).

Evening ticket (from 4.30 PM): £12.00 (two-fish limit).
Junior ticket (Under 16): £16.00 (full day, three-fish limit); £12.50 (half day, two-fish limit).

For more information contact: Barrie Bawden, Avon Springs Fishing Lakes, Recreation Road, Durrington, Salisbury, Wiltshire. Telephone: (0980) 53557.

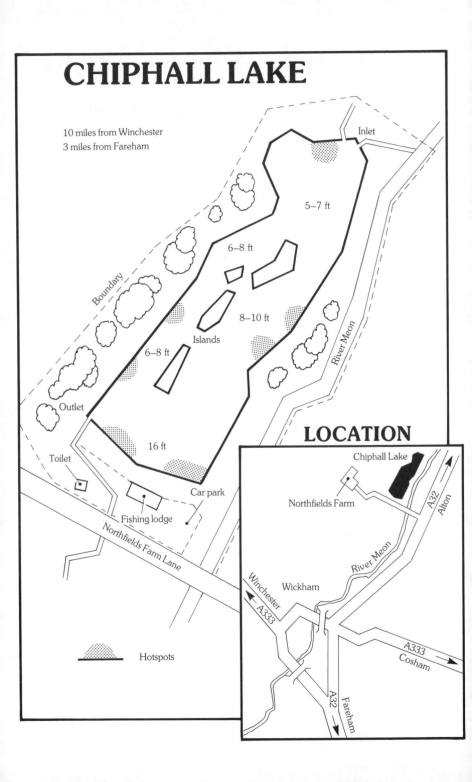

CHIPHALL LAKE

Many new trout waters are opening up, but few have earned a reputation for productivity as fast as Chiphall. This fishery is located in the prized Meon valley in southern Hampshire, one of the last strongholds against the developers and something of a wildlife refuge. The Meon valley is a popular tourist route, and the fishery, located off the A32 near Wickham, is in the heart of the countryside yet in easy reach of the larger towns. The tiny River Meon, which burbles and chuckles its way through the valley, is so small you would not realize that it is probably the third-best trout stream in southern England. It seems to be little more than a ditch, but as it increases in size it looks more fit for fish and is in fact one of the purest sources of water in the South.

To find the fishery, drive north-east from Wickham on the A32 towards Alton. About ¾ mile outside Wickham is a track on your left called Northfields Farm Lane, and if you look out for this you will undoubtedly spot the lake. You will probably be almost on top of the lane before you realize it, and as this is a fast stretch of road I suggest that you go further up and turn round, rather than brake hard and reverse.

Botley is about 5 miles away, Alton 14 miles, and Fareham and the link to the M27 just 3 miles. Access could not be easier. The fishery is on the Rookesbury Estate and was dug out in the early 1980s with the specific purpose of providing trout fishing. The main problem with the initial excavation was that the depth was too shallow for trout. This meant that water temperatures would rise very quickly in a hot summer, reducing the oxygen content, which stresses the trout or even kills them. Equally, with a hard winter the lake might freeze from top to bottom, and the trout are lost that way. Now, under the new leaseholder, Marilyn Madsen, the lake has been deepened and landscaped to provide a first-class environment for both trout and anglers. The water feed is via an inflow straight from the Meon. When I last visited, the volume was considerable and pushed out some distance into the lake. Marilyn has been interested in the sport for the last five years, and fishermen not acquainted with the venue might be pleasantly surprised to be greeted by an attractive blonde who was previously a freelance in the fashion industry in Oxford Street. Marilyn opened Chiphall in the 1988 season, and while the initial stocking policy had a target average of 2 lb, the end-of-season tally saw this figure reach 3 lb.

To illustrate the high average weight, that first season saw 293 fish caught, ranging between 5 lb and 12½ lb. The eight double-figure fish recorded fell as follows: Mr Williams, 12½ lb; Dr Brewer, 12½ lb; Stuart Hunter, 11 lb 10 oz; David Mitchell, 10 lb 14 oz; Alan Grant, 10 lb 4 oz; D. Griffiths, 10 lb 2 oz; B. Rowden and H. Burgess, 10 lb each. The largest brown trout fell to Alan Grant and weighed 7 lb. There were also a number of four-fish-limit bags that beat the 20 lb mark.

There was a slight problem with the road and car park, which became tacky when it rained, but both have now been successfully reinforced. Also, there was the start of a weed problem, but the water level was dropped during the winter and the worst of the marginal weed killed off. This latter problem was undoubtedly a result of those years when the lake remained shallow and the weed took a strong hold in the summer heat.

Marilyn could not afford to advertise during her opening season, having spent a lot on deepening the lake and landscaping. However, she has retained a hard core of trouting enthusiasts among the season-ticket holders, who remained with her once the water had settled down and good catches had become the norm. The lake is at present around five acres and can be fished from all the banks, which have been cleared for easy casting. In addition to the Meon, two springs also supplement the water. The river rises above Meonstoke, changing from virtually a ditch to a tiny stream, to run into the sea at Titchfield. Sea trout run up to the mill at Wickham, and a few make it beyond that.

APPROACH AND TACKLE

Water depths now average around 7–8 ft – ideal for the trout and also for the fly-fishing enthusiast, who can present the fish with an offering on the surface, in the surface film, at mid-water, or right on the bottom. Such rich, pollution-free water, gives a maximum yield of insect life, and it is no surprise to learn of the wide choice available. There are very good damselfly, corixa, buzzers, shrimps, and lots of

Two rainbows and a brown for John Nicholson from Basingstoke. He used a Damsel nymph on a floating line coupled to a long leader for a delicate presentation. It was his first trip to Chiphall.

Floating lines are the order of the day at Chiphall Lake. In summer both dry fly and surface nymphs score very well.

snail and mayfly. The mayfly season is short, and, as is the case in much of the area, does not boast a truly thick traditional hatch. Certainly, in May or June it is worth keeping an eye open for them. Any cool winds blowing down this valley put the insects down, but once the wind drops or becomes very light they start hatching again.

Chiphall is turning into a very good dry-fly water, possibly because of its location in this valley. The surface can alternate hourly between flat calm and ripply, the best conditions for hatching insects. The water has three islands, and the angler casting to the edge of them will do particularly well with the dry fly. If conditions allow, you should aim to put the fly in the lee of any island, dropping it very tight to the edge, where the bigger trout will be cruising. The dam area in front of the lodge is the favourite with both dry-fly and sunk-line anglers, particularly the right-hand corner as you look at the lake from the lodge. The depth here drops away to about 16 ft and you can get down with a sinking line on those hot, bright days when surface activity dies off. There is one small island that appears to serve no purpose except as a duck platform, and Marilyn hopes to have this removed for the 1990 season.

The 1989 season started the way the previous season finished, with the average fish weight running at 2½ lb and the fish-per-rod average at 3, which is very high indeed. The trout are all in tip-top condition, having been supplied by Itchen Valley Trout Farm, which rears fish at Alresford on spring water and has a reputation among fishery owners for providing good, clean stockfish. Stocking is undertaken at least three times per week, more if demand dictates it. Anglers might also be interested to learn that the reason the surface is clear from weed when they get there is because Marilyn and her workers will have been busy since the crack of dawn preparing the venue and clearing weed with a line of chained logs!

SEASONAL TACTICS

As this is a relatively new fishery there are many fly-fishing options to experiment with. However, my seasonal advice is as follows.

Spring

If the previous winter has been cold, try a fast-sink line with a greased leader and a buoyant fly. There are very few trees, so twigs and leaves should be no problem. The fisherman retrieving the fly slowly will score over the fast stripper. Viva and Appetiser are local favourites in early spring. If it warms up, change to a slow-sink, and if you see the odd fish or two showing, try the floating line. Small nymphs will come into their own in May, and with a breeze you should try the dam area.

Summer

This is the time to get the best of the surface fishing. If you prefer dry fly, try to match any hatch, but be sure to use small flies. There is not a large mayfly hatch, and I would only use this pattern if you can see the trout taking them. In very breezy weather, especially with a south-westerly airflow, it will be best to fish a slow-sink line. Remember, the weed growth on the bottom will now be at its most active, and you should isolate your fly just over the top of it, rather than in it. Now is the time to start spotting individual fish, particularly in the corners of the lake by the dam, or near the islands.

Target-casting to the points of the islands with either a dry fly or a slow-sinking nymph can be rewarding, but fish everything slowly. If a lot of anglers have been hammering the water before you, try to make a mental note of how fast they were retrieving. Success when things start to go quiet is not necessarily due to a change of fly pattern, but a change of retrieve speeds. Slowing everything down often evokes a response from the trout.

Autumn

There are plenty of brown trout in Chiphall, and plenty of minnows for them to feed on. To most anglers this situation suggests mini lures or big nymphs fished on a slow-sink line in the margins. At the top end of the lake is the substantial inflow from the Meon. This is a recognized hot-spot for browns, and you would do well to concentrate your sub-surface efforts here. Try the points of the islands as well, since those bigger browns are invariably territorial, and the minnows will be around the island margins as well. The dry-fly man will find plenty to amuse himself with if he fishes the Daddy Longlegs on September evenings, when the damp makes them active.

GENERAL INFORMATION

Chiphall has adequate car parking, toilet facilities, and a small clubhouse. It is hoped to construct a further six or seven-acre lake below the dam level of the first. This will boost the number of rods available, 12 at present, and offer far more scope to the fly fisherman. Barbecues can be arranged, and block bookings are taken for groups or clubs. If you can get 12 (or more) anglers together, you can have your own fishing party and take over Chiphall for the day. Corporate and bulk bookings also enjoy a 10 per cent discount for advance booking and payment.

No visitors are allowed, as Marilyn wants to keep Chiphall a strictly sportfishing venue, and the rules to this end are very basic. Fishing is with fly and nymph only, with a single hook of maximum size 10, and a fly length not to exceed 1 in. All fish are to be retained. Rod limits must be strictly adhered to. On reaching the limit the angler must stop fishing until another ticket is purchased. No rod sharing is allowed. Fishing starts at 9 AM, but see the notice at the fishing lodge for details of closing times. A Southern Water Authority licence is required.

Prices for 1990 are as follows:

Day ticket: £22.50 (four-fish limit).
Half-day ticket: £13.50 (two-fish limit).
Evening tickets: by appointment only. It is best to phone on the day to check availability.
Full-season rod (one named day per week): £520.00 (four-fish limit).
Half-season rod (one named day per fortnight): £275.00 (four-fish limit).
Books of tickets are available at a 10 per cent discount.

For more information contact: Marilyn Madsen, Chiphall Lake Trout Fishery, 12 Victoria Buildings, Winchester Road, Bishops Waltham, Hampshire, SO3 1BG. Telephone: (0329) 833295 or (0489) 894845 outside of fishing hours.

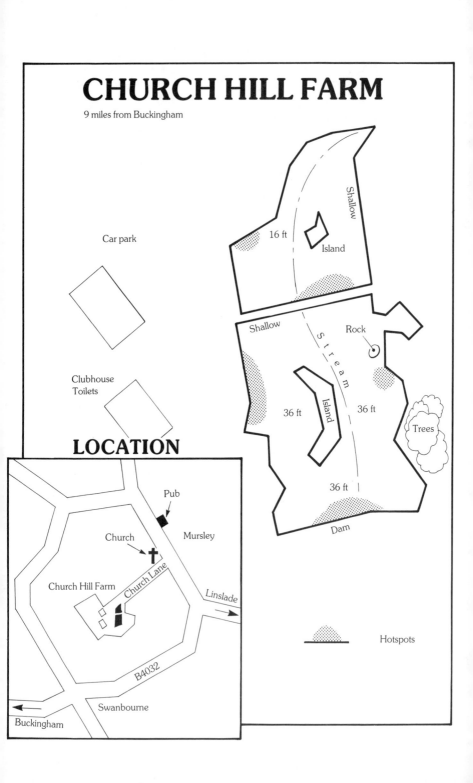

CHURCH HILL FARM

9 miles from Buckingham

Car park

Shallow

16 ft

Island

Shallow

Rock

Stream

Clubhouse
Toilets

36 ft

Island

36 ft

Trees

LOCATION

36 ft

Dam

Pub

Mursley

Church

Church Hill Farm

Church Lane

Linslade

B4032

Swanbourne

Buckingham

Hotspots

CHURCH HILL FARM

This venue is one of the longer-established small water trout fisheries and has produced a constant string of good fish. In a valley in the heart of Buckinghamshire's quiet farmland lie the two lakes of Church Hill Farm. There is provision for a new lake to be constructed on adjacent land, and this may well be finished for the start of the 1990 trout season. Only some 50 miles from Central London, the fishery is well established, with a reputation that has grown steadily, not least for winning the prestigious 'Salmon and Trout behind the scenes' award. Church Hill Farm was first opened to fishermen in 1977, and in 1978 the old clubhouse was opened, offering lunches that used provisions supplied by the farm grounds. The fishery is just outside the village of Mursley, which is west of Leighton Buzzard and south-east of Buckingham.

Built exclusively for trout fishing, the lakes were formed by damming a small stream that ran through the valley. This stream is the beginning of the River Ouse and still runs through the bed of both lakes. The smaller Dog Lake was the first to be built, and was followed by the second, opened in 1977, which gives this larger water its name, Jubilee Lake. Owner Tim Daniels was in at the very start of the construction. A keen angler himself, his aim was always to offer the discerning fly fisherman good sport at a competitive price.

Experienced angler and novice alike have a good chance of finding a fish or two, since the lakes have a fair stocking of medium to large fish. There are shallows, secluded bays which the trout sneak into on quiet days, and deep water that provides cover for the fish during the cold winter months. Many shallow waters have the disadvantage of cooling too rapidly in spring and autumn, when clear nights allow the heat to radiate out. Equally, though, a shallow water can warm up quickly and bring the trout on the feed much faster than a deep water. Weighing up the pros and cons, and bearing in mind our fluctuating weather, I feel that deeper water, with its constant temperature range, gives better sport over a longer period.

The smaller Dog Leg Lake is about two and a half acres and

provides comfortable fishing from all banks. The water is alkaline, owing to the Ouse feeder stream, and holds an abundance of insect life. The deep water tends to run down the centre, following the bed of the old stream, and dropping to 16 ft along this channel. The north-east bank is shallow, and two popular hot-spots are marked on the map. With deep water close in, the bigger trout will tend to range along the drop off, venturing up into the shallows only very early in the morning. Often the angler first at the water in the morning will take the biggest fish. With good eating facilities supplied by Tim there is similarly a period at lunchtime when some areas of the bank are deserted. It only takes 15–20 minutes' rest from the continual criss-crossing of anglers' lines for the trout to settle down. If you fish at this time you can often pick up those trout that had previously seemed impossible, particularly the bigger-than-average fish.

Jubilee Lake is larger, around seven and a half acres, with a narrow island running down the centre. The central bed of the Ouse feeder stream runs deepest through the middle of the lake, and trout can be caught at the amazing depth of 36 ft. This fact should be borne in mind in very hot weather, when most fish will go deeper to take advantage of the higher oxygen content and stable temperature. In the west corner of Jubilee Lake, and in the centre of the dam, you can put a 15-yard line straight out into over 30 ft of water. The east bank is shallow, and allows some stalking of fish in windless conditions.

Stocking is undertaken on a daily basis, using both browns and rainbows up to double figures, although the average weight is much nearer 2 lb. Tim puts his stocking level at somewhere between 8000 and 10,000 fish per year. At the time of writing, the fishery record for brown trout stands at 9 lb 12 oz, and for the rainbow at 15 lb 4 oz. The browns in particular seem to like the deeper water and are often in good condition, providing excellent autumn fishing. Fry will move into the margins and shallows, inviting the use of a variety of fry-imitating lures.

APPROACH AND TACKLE

The rich alkaline water accounts for an abundance of insect life that will keep most anglers flicking through their fly wallets. While fish will always be caught with the throw-it-out-and-pull-it-back approach, more will be landed in the difficult periods if you try to get a grasp of the insect life blooming at that particular time of year. For fishing near

Youngster Robin Evans used floating line and a Viva lure in the small lake at Church Hill Farm to take this 1½ lb fish.

the bottom you can use orange or green shrimps, there being an abundance of shrimp in the water. Snails will also form part of the brown trout's diet, and again you should fish near the bottom.

Nearer the surface you will need to use either a slow-sink or an intermediate line and to fish with corixa and buzzers. Black or green are good colours on most waters and work well at Church Hill Farm. Other natural insects worth following are sedge, damselfly, and hawthorn. Church Hill enjoys a long mayfly season – up to six weeks and peaking as late as mid-June. Obviously the Mayfly nymph will work well in this period, but try the Gold Ribbed Hare's Ear as a standby. The lakes, located as they are in the middle of farmland, enjoy well-established bird life. There can be both Canada and Brent geese, plus a variety of ducks such as mallard, diving and tufted. There are several kingfishers, and foxes are often seen by early-morning fishermen, as are the Muntjac deer that drink at the lakeside.

SEASONAL TACTICS

Spring

Cold weather is more likely to affect the fishermen than it does the fish. With depths of over 30 ft available, the trout will simply swim deeper, where the temperature range is more constant. For that reason, fish the dam wall of Jubilee Lake with a fast-sink line, but grease the leader and use a buoyant pop-up nymph, fishing it back slowly over the bottom. Then try a slow-sink line with a very slow retrieve, using the countdown technique to search out the different feeding layers of the trout. The Leech fly is also good for fishing the edge of the drop off. In late April you have the hawthorn fly, but do not neglect the Viva, Montana or lead-headed lures.

Summer

The full cycle of natural insects will now be at their peak. In mid-June you will still have plenty of hawthorns and mayfly to imitate. Fishing in the surface film you can capitalize by using both sedges and buzzers. Select either an intermediate or slow-sink line for this. The floating line and dry fly will be good late in the evening when there is a very light ripple on the water. Suspender buzzers have also produced well for the last few years. Visual stalking of individual cruising trout can also be done, but the banks are open, so once you spot a fish try to keep a low profile against the skyline. For casting to

Sidney Mears from Streatham, London, took this rainbow from the dam wall of the main lake at Church Hill Farm. It took a lure on a slow-fished sinking line.

Fishing the dam wall at Church Hill Farm seems to produce rainbows regularly.

these bigger cruising fish you need a heavily weighted nymph such as a Mayfly or Damsel, and you should present the fly to the fish about 6 ft from where it is cruising. When the trout gets near, slowly tweak the fly away from it. Watch for the mouth opening and strike when you see the fish turn away. The smaller Dog Leg Lake is slightly better for dry fly in the summer and has a greater selection of natural insect life.

Autumn

There are plenty of sticklebacks in the margins, so try a Church Fry lure, Baby Doll or Jersey Herd as an imitator. On the surface the Daddy Longlegs is a favourite autumn method, working best when there is a slight breeze. One of the best places to try this is from the dam on Jubilee Lake when a warm south-westerly breeze allows you to drift it far out near the island.

GENERAL INFORMATION

In addition to the new lake, a brand new clubhouse was scheduled to be built late in 1989. Lunches can be pre-booked for your day of fishing, and are the main reason why the lakes get such a rest around midday! The clubhouse at present also holds an extensive collection of mounted fish and historic old tackle, of which many collectors would be deeply envious. This includes line driers, Hardy reels, and brown trout, rainbow trout, brook trout, bream, pike and roach in cases. The Church Hill Farm club is open to all for a £10 joining fee and £25 per year subscription. There is a comprehensive tackle shop where you can stock up on all the necessary equipment: rods, reels, nets, flies and leaders, and clothing. Some of the flies are tied specially for use at Church Hill Farm. Tackle can be hired at £3.00 per day and comprises rod, reel, net, etc. Leaders and flies must be purchased separately. There is also a weighing room and all catches must be recorded. If you are a beginner you can get casting and fishing tuition for £7 per hour. There are adequate parking and toilet facilities, and the family are allowed to come but not to go near the lakes. Children under 14 are allowed to share an adult's permit if they are beginners.

Tim also likes to offer the very best in corporate fishing days. Coffee is served on arrival, followed by pre-lunch drinks, a three- or four-course lunch with wines, and afternoon tea. The party – minimum 20, maximum 30 – will have the exclusive use of the fishery and all its facilities throughout the day. Prices for this, including the fishing ticket, are £30–40 per head inclusive. Some of the companies using Church Hill Farm on the corporate days enjoy the beauty of the surrounding farmland as well as some excellent fishing. There is also a discount for bulk club bookings of up to 30 anglers.

Prices for the fishery are as follows:

Day ticket: £18.50
Half-day ticket: £10.00

For more information contact: Tim Daniels, Church Hill Farm, Mursley, Buckinghamshire. Telephone: Mursley (029672) 524.

DORSET SPRINGS LAKES

4 miles from Wimborne Minster
5 miles from Poole

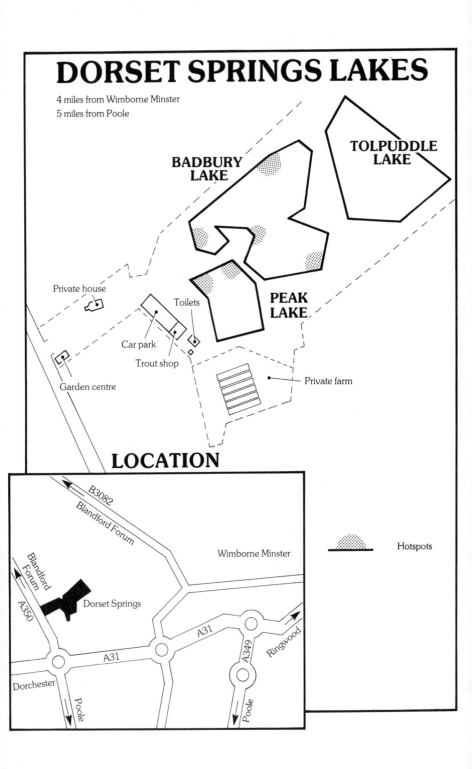

TOLPUDDLE LAKE

BADBURY LAKE

PEAK LAKE

Private house

Toilets

Car park

Trout shop

Garden centre

Private farm

LOCATION

B3082
Blandford Forum

Blandford Forum

A350

Dorset Springs

Wimborne Minster

A31

A31

A349

Ringwood

Dorchester

Poole

Poole

Hotspots

DORSET SPRINGS LAKES

With Dorset making its mark on the fly-fishing world with a number of good fisheries, I feel that it is worth mentioning another good water in the south of this county. Dorset Springs Lakes is a trout fishery with a difference. Whereas many fisheries are aimed exclusively at the fly-fishing market, this is a commercial venture with a positive leaning towards being a leisure complex. We are all by now aware of how we follow in the footsteps of the United States. With the increase in leisure time comes a subsequent growth in the leisure market, as has happened across the Atlantic.

This fishery offers the angler a unique combination of very accessible fishing for both trout and coarse fish. Indeed, there are plans to expand even further, to offer fishermen more facilities and a greater acreage of water. Located close to the historic town of Wimborne Minster, the complex, owned by Mr Brayne, was first dug back in 1981. At that stage he had left the construction industry and ventured into the world of fish farming. Those first excavations were carried out to expand the hatchery side of the business and to make provision for three lakes. Two of these are given over to fly fishing, one being five acres, the other one acre. There is also a lake of three acres adjacent to the other two, providing sport for the coarse fisherman.

The first lake, near the entrance, is around 15 ft deep and quite clear. The second lake has a mixture of deeps and shallows, allowing the angler an interesting choice of techniques. Depths here range from 6 ft down to 18 ft. Owing to the depth of the water there are few major weed problems, yet there is enough weed to provide a sheltered habitat for the insect life. The mayfly hatch in particular is very good, by virtue of the stream that runs alongside the hatchery farm.

The property lies on the edge of the flood plains of the Dorset

Stour, and is centred on 54 acres of farmland. With a rod limit of just 20 fly fishermen, there is plenty of space to move around and try the points and bays where the rainbows might be cruising. The lakes are spring-fed, going clear in the summer months. Insect life is prolific: as well as the mayfly, you have hawthorn, sedge, buzzer and damsel to work with. The mayfly hatch can be excellent, but a little short-lived. The first two weeks of June are best. This insect's numbers always tend to fluctuate, and a cold winter coupled to a late spring invariably minimizes their activities. Yet a few warm winters, like those we have had recently, may see them become more established at Dorset Springs.

The trout farm itself was constructed in 1986 to supply the restaurant trade and obtains about 76 tons of trout per year, with the outlet being only through their own farm shop and the fishery. Having its own hatchery, Dorset Springs has the option of separating the faster-growing rainbows for feeding on to stock the lakes. This high productivity is maintained by pure bore-hole water, although there are no plans for further expansion of the fish farm.

The expansion scheme on this property includes the development of another two lakes, one of seven acres, the other of a generous 13 acres. These will have a fairly even depth of 18 ft, with odd banks of shallow water to provide interesting fishing features. The trout farm that stocks the lakes also offers a catch-your-meal pond, where anyone wanting to buy trout for a meal can hire a rod from the rack and catch them fresh! I have found this commonplace when I have travelled in the United States, and it often proves a highly popular sideline. It draws wives and children like a magnet, with youngsters seeming to take great delight in despatching the trout with an enthusiasm that would surely be admired by the horror-movie directors! For these trout you pay £1.50 per pound, although prices are obviously subject to the market value. Tackle is hired, together with a supply of shrimps for hookbait.

APPROACH AND TACKLE

No large lures are allowed, particularly the lead-headed variety, and fly dressing is limited to an overall length of 1 in. There are no fry in the water, so there is no need to think about fry-feeding autumnal fish in the margins. No browns are stocked in the lakes, only rainbows from the fishery's own farm, with specimens into double figures. The fishery record at the time of writing stands at 10 lb 6 oz.

On the main lake an angler slides the net under a fighting Dorset Springs rainbow, taken on a floating line.

While nymphs can be productive at any time of the year, it should be noted that dry-fly activity peaks during the normally difficult months of June, July and August. Small nymphs will also fish a lot better than large nymphs, and you are allowed to drop your leader strength in order to make a better presentation of either dry fly or buzzer.

SEASONAL TACTICS

This is a year-round venue with a constant depth of water, and so seasonal advice would be of limited value. However, these guidelines may be of assistance.

Spring

Start with a sinking line and large nymphs, fishing them slowly near the bottom. Use the countdown technique to search out the water layers until you locate feeding fish. Cover the deep, open water during the day in cold weather, then concentrate more on the bays in April.

Anglers work the bank on the large lake at Dorset Springs, searching the depths to find the feeding rainbows.

Summer

In early June try staying on into the evening to take advantage of any mayfly that might be hatching. In late June, and through July and August, concentrate your attentions in the upper 3 ft of water, fishing a floating line, 3 lb leader and a buzzer, Pheasant Tail or corixa, retrieved slowly. The water is clear, so try to keep a good distance from any trout, and use a very long leader of at least 10–12 ft. Check your hook point every so often in case it catches the bank behind you on a back cast. Go through the basic dry-fly colours of dark green, brown or black in hook sizes of 12 to 14. Late evening is the best time for dry fly.

Autumn

Fish exactly the same as you would in the summer. In September very small nymphs will fish well, but October may see a drop in the water temperature and larger, weighted nymph patterns will be useful. There will be only a slight drop in surface temperature, so stay with the floating line, but speed up your retrieve a bit.

Winter

All you need do now is to stay with the larger nymphs, but change to a slow-sink line and speed up your retrieve slightly. Do not spend too much time in one place. Half an hour should be enough, then move to another spot. Watch out for takes close to the bank, since in winter fish often follow a fly some distance before taking.

GENERAL INFORMATION

There is adequate car parking, toilets, picnic and barbecue areas, a hot and cold drinks dispenser and other refreshments. The rules are fairly basic: fly fishing only with a single hook, maximum size No. 8. All fish caught are to be killed; no fish is to be returned to the water. All fish must be weighed in on completion of fishing and recorded in the log book. Nil returns are also to be recorded, so you must call in at the ticket office before leaving. There is no tackle shop at present, but one is proposed in the expansion programme scheduled for 1990. Flies, leaders and other tackle will be available. However, fishery instruction is available now at a rate of £7.50 per angler per hour, with rod hire extra. The latter comprises a rod, reel, line and net for £3.00 per day, with flies and leaders extra. In 1988 the

How's this for a first-time catch? This youngster tried the catch-and-buy pond using shrimp as bait and came up with this fine rainbow.

fish-per-rod average was very good, at 2.6. The rainbows averaged about 2½ lb. All fishermen purchasing tickets must report to the fishery manager before beginning to fish. Children under 14 years of age must be accompanied by an adult. A bonus here is that you are allowed to take one guest, who can share the rod. This allows an experienced angler the chance to teach a beginner or friend the art of trout fishing at a shared cost. Wading is not allowed. Purchase of a ticket is regarded as an agreement to abide by the fishery rules. The fishery is open from 8 AM to dusk all year, except for Christmas Day and Boxing Day.

The ticket prices are as follows:

Day ticket: £16.00 (five-fish limit).
Half-day ticket (either morning or afternoon): £12.00 (four-fish limit).
Evening ticket: £10 (three-fish limit).
Junior prices (under 14) are: Day ticket: £12.00 (four-fish limit).
Half-day: £10 (three-fish limit).
Evening ticket: £8.00 (two-fish limit).
Season and half-season tickets are available on request. Dorset Springs offers discounts for both club and corporate bookings, but this arrangement is limited to weekdays.

For more information contact: Mr Butterworth, Dorset Springs Lakes, Poole Road, Sturminster Marshall, Nr Wimborne, Dorset BH21 4AE. Telephone: Sturminster Marshall (0258) 857653.

HALLIFORD MERE

5 miles from Staines
2 miles from Chertsey

Clubhouse

Car park

Driveway

20 ft

30 ft

Islands

Main island

20 ft

18–20 ft

12–18 ft

Gravel causeways

Three Trees
bank

LOCATION

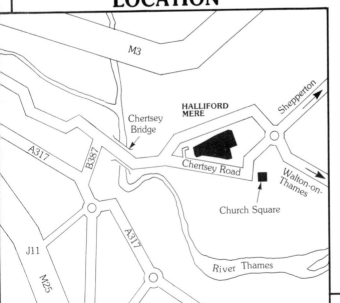

M3

HALLIFORD
MERE

Shepperton

Chertsey
Bridge

A317

B387

Chertsey Road

Walton-on-
Thames

Church Square

J11

A317

M25

River Thames

Hotspots

HALLIFORD MERE

Finding a venue very near to London is surely a boon to anglers who work there. Usually you can forget about grabbing the odd half day at a trout fishery, because of the distance involved. Now, with the recent opening of the Halliford Mere Fly Fishery at Shepperton, near the Middlesex/Surrey border, the fisherman working in London can leave work at lunchtime and be casting a fly on tranquil waters by 2 PM. The creation of this highly convenient fishery was the brainchild of brothers Bill and Robin Berwick. They envisage the venue being highly popular, mainly because of its proximity to the M25 and London's West End and City.

A half-acre pond was the only original connection with anything remotely fishy. This was at the western end of the property. About 25 years ago gravel was extracted for the construction of the nearby motorway system, and it was not until then that this waste ground began to realize its potential as a fishery. The gravel company broke into several springs in its search for gravel, and finally finished its work some five years ago when the lagoon in the north-east corner was dug out. The water in this gravel working was left to naturalize and develop its own ecosystem. A local angling club took possession, but only on a short lease. Then the Berwick brothers happened along, and purchased the property in 1985.

Bill and Robin went through the formalities of analysing the soil and the oxygen content, receiving a lot of help from the Thames Water Authority, although they went to the Severn-Trent Water Authority for a second opinion. They already had a fair idea of the shape of the gravel bed, but in 1986 they sent down a team of divers to establish where the weedbeds were, what depths shelved up and where, where the gravel beds were in relation to the banks, and which areas had silted up. Using wrist gauges, the divers recorded an average depth of around 20 ft, with a few holes dropping away to 35 ft.

This sort of depth meant that the brothers had the potential for overwintering a lot of trout, and that in heat waves in the summer there would be a much reduced risk of mortalities among the stock. The first stocking took place in April 1987 and comprised rainbow trout ranging from 1½ lb to 7½ lb. Two batches of 700 fish each were put in, all purchased from Bridge Farm Hatcheries near Basingstoke. These were left to settle in until the fishery opened in August 1987, after which the owners topped up the stock once a week. There is also an outside chance of hooking one of the natural browns that live in the water. Generally, these range from 1½ lb to 2½ lb, but a number of trout fishermen have seen double-figure browns, perhaps as large as 12 lb. Many fishermen have been broken up by these monster fish, which we can only assume live happily in the cool of the deep water. The fish-per-rod average stands at about 2½, but it is the ticket distribution pattern that makes this water interesting. A survey revealed that in the summer up to 80 per cent of all tickets sold are for afternoon and evening fishing, which would seem to confirm the fishery's popularity among those who take advantage of the easy access from London.

Rather than make it too easy, the owners arrange the stocking in such a way that there is always a challenge. The water's clarity means that even though it is deep you can stalk individual fish on this year-round fishery. The depths, quite apart from any rules, preclude the use of waders, but you can in fact reach three of the islands set in the middle of the lake by means of a gravel causeway. This was not intentional, but is the result of the gravel company using an extraction technique called 'throwback'. As a result, the angler can wade over the causeway, select a piece of island and work his flies straight into the deep water. There are no real hot-spots, but the islands are a favoured area. And do not forget to look along the edge of the causeway before you wade out. Very often trout will be working in the shallow water, so try for any you see first, before you wade out and spook them.

The total water area is about 15 acres and the distance, should you wish to walk round the lake, is just over a mile. The fishery is long and narrow, which makes it ideal when a breeze puts a ripple on the water, since any surface-borne food is carried down its entire length, to finish up on one of the islands. There are no real hot-spots – the water holds fish throughout its whole length. Wildlife was quick to become established in such high-quality water, and grebes, ducks, moorhens, coots and swans are all to be seen.

The worst wind direction is a northerly, which restricts your back cast from the lodge bank, and is too strong for the forward cast on the

Richard Johnstone used a floating line and an Appetiser lure in the bay directly in front of the lodge: a good hot-spot just 20 yards from the car park!

facing bank. The prevailing south-westerly airflow is the most productive, and puts a good ripple on the whole lake. Since the fishery is long and narrow, and also has several islands, there are still places that offer flat calm conditions.

APPROACH AND TACKLE

The venue is ideal for two distinct types of fisherman. The first type are quite happy to fish directly into the teeth of the wind, knowing full well that this is where most of the food will be. The trout soon capitalize on this approach and will take a fly fished very close to the bank. You can either cast straight out into the wind and wait for a take until the last few yards of your retrieve, or you can cast at 45

An angler slides the net under a rainbow at Halliford Mere. There are no monsters in this lake, but the water quality is excellent and action is never far away.

degrees to the bank, and put your fly through a larger area of feeding zone. If you adopt the latter tactic, remember that the chances of getting a hook stuck in some part of your anatomy are considerably increased during windy weather. If you are a right-handed caster you can reduce this risk by standing with the wind over your left shoulder (vice versa if you are left-handed). This simply ensures that the wind blows the line away from you, rather than pushes it towards you.

The other main type of angler at Halliford is the dry-fly specialist. These fishermen are quite happy to take fish from the open water in a steady ripple, but find that during strong wind the calm areas under bank lees or below the islands suit their style better. For some reason there are always plenty of trout in these flat calm places, so never neglect them too soon.

Since Halliford is a relatively new water it is unwise to make a snap assessment of it. At the time of writing, the fishery record for brown trout stands at 12 lb, and there are plenty more of those big wild browns lurking in the deeper water. The rainbow trout record is well over 9 lb, and several fish stocked have yet to reach double figures. The largest overwintered fish came out at over 8 lb, and the most fish taken in one day by an angler was 27. Of the limit bags, the heaviest I know of weighed 2¾ lb, 4¼ lb, 5 lb 14 oz, and 7 lb 2 oz.

As for insect life, the water has a profusion of mayfly. Usually these turn up very late, sometimes two weeks later than at other venues. However, they also tend to stay longer, up to four weeks or so, into July. Needless to say, the surface fishing at that time is of top quality. There are lots of sedges, at least four different varieties, as well as

There are plenty of gravel bars and islands which mark the deeps and the shallows. Here an angler fishes a gravel bar for shallow-feeding fish, while the boat angler searches out deeper-feeding trout.

The boats at Halliford are top quality and allow the anglers to get away from any bankside activity.

This 2 lb 9 oz rainbow came to a Canadian nymph fished on a sink-tip line near the lodge. Captor was Shepperton angler Robert Cook, on only his second visit to Halliford Mere.

damsels and the usual midges, gnats and daddy longlegs. The olives can fish reasonably well; they are certainly there, although not in abundance. The best of the surface fishing is with the Mayfly in June and early July, and then the Daddy Longlegs into late September and early October.

Lures work well in the deeper water, but I feel that it is better to find the depth and speed at which the trout are taking, rather than go too deep and miss them. This is often a problem for sinking-line enthusiasts, who usually subscribe to the fallacy that all big trout are way down in the dark and cold depths. In fact at Halliford Mere there are two distinct types of feeding fish. There are the rainbows that actually work in the surface film, which are best approached with a dry fly or buzzer fished in it. Then there are the trout working at a depth of around 2 ft, which respond best to a slow-retrieve standard nymph pattern or a small lure. To reach those places that even the long caster cannot get to, you need one of the boats. Three are available, and they can be moored up to buoys at pre-anchored marks, thus avoiding any conflict between boat and bank anglers. A boat costs £5.00 for a half day or an evening session, or £8.00 for a full day, and will take up to two anglers.

There are very few restrictions at this fishery. You can even fish with a team of flies, something banned at many small waters. One of the more popular Halliford teams combines Buzzer, Damsel and Invicta. Double hooks and Pennell tackle are banned, and 5 lb is the recommended minimum tippet strength. However, if you have to go to the lengths of imitating caenis in those dog days of summer, then you are allowed to drop below this strength.

SEASONAL TACTICS

Spring

Use a floating line, and a very long leader, at least 10 ft and possibly up to 15 ft. Any black nymph scores well, and Pheasant Tails, Muddler, Mayfly, Booby, Black and Peacock and Tadpoles fished slow are the Halliford favourites. The heaviest line you will need is only a sink-tip, but use a weighted nymph to get down. Most of the fish are in the top 4 ft of water at this time of year.

Summer

Those searching the layer of water extending from the surface to 3 ft deep should try small Baby Dolls, Gold Ribbed Hare's Ear, Dragonfly and other standard nymphs. The standard wet-fly patterns also work very well, notably the Teal and Blue, Butcher, March Brown, and then the various sedge pupae. A slow to medium retrieve is best, and rarely does any fast stripping produce. But then again fish can be particular, so never be afraid to try something different if takes are slow. On and in the surface film you can offer nymphs: Dry Hare's Ear, Mayfly, Mallard and Claret, and Cove.

Autumn and Winter

I have dealt with these two seasons together as the water is so deep that the water temperature is likely to remain fairly constant. Even into early October and November the Dry Sedge or Daddy Longlegs will produce. When it gets really cold you can switch to a Montana, Baby Doll, Appetiser or orange lure. There are many coarse fish fry in Halliford, which is probably why the smaller lures work so well. Throughout the worst of the winter it is best to consult the catch returns to see which have been the most productive patterns over the previous couple of days.

GENERAL INFORMATION

There is an ample car park just adjacent to a main road, with subsequent easy access to the M25. The clubhouse has a male/female WC and even boasts a fire. Should anything more effective than the fire be required to warm you, the bar will cater for your needs. Built by Bill and Robin from ground plans, the clubhouse has a perfect view of the lake over a grassy slope. Future plans involve selling tackle, and barbecues in the summer. The brothers hold several charity functions each season and have already raised quite a bit of money for Guide Dogs for the Blind. Casting and fishing tuition is available at £10.00 per hour for either individuals or groups.

1990 ticket prices are:

Day ticket: £18.00 (five-fish limit).
Halfday ticket (8 AM–1 PM or 1 PM until dusk): £13.00 (three-fish limit).
Evening ticket: £10.00 (two-fish limit). The evening ticket is in fact for a four-hour session that can be taken at any time of the day, and is by far the most popular choice.

Any fish over the standard limit can be purchased by the pound as you leave the fishery.

For more information contact: Bill or Robin Berwick, Halliford Mere Club, Chertsey Road, Shepperton, Middlesex TW17 9EG. Telephone: (0932) 248547.

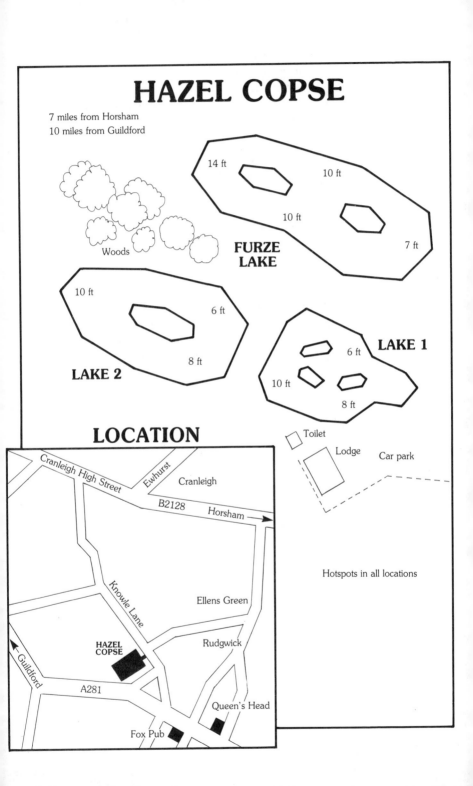

HAZEL COPSE

Located off the A281 between Guildford and Horsham, the venue known as Hazel Copse is surely destined to be a leading trout water of the future. Located in Surrey, near the border with Sussex, where the countryside still stands moderately protected from the ravages of the developer, Hazel Copse produces an amazing number of brown trout, rainbow trout and stillwater salmon. Some of the finest views in England can be seen from the edge of Guildford along the ridge of hills known as the Hog's Back. The area between Rudgwick and Buck's Green on this stretch of the A281 has many small woods and copses. It is home to much wildlife, and owing to the wealth of woodland there are many yellowhammers and woodpeckers. In the surrounding open countryside, skylarks abound.

The fishery's owner, Wilf Welch, originally bought the land to put his beef cattle on, but finding some of it to be damp, he decided instead to go in for a trout fishery. He explained to me that there is little difference between looking after animals and fish, for their care is based on similar principles. Mr Welch runs the fishery with his wife, and work began some five years ago when the first lake was dug. This was not excavated with a long-armed Hymac excavation digger – the usual method. Mr Welch works fast once he has decided to do something, and used bulldozers to scour out the lake bed.

The surrounding soil is heavy clay, so there was no question of the lake not holding water. Moreover, despite this clay base, the water in the first lake is remarkable in being gin-clear. Many clay-bottomed lakes have a milky colour as a result of water running off the land. The lake was stocked with trout almost immediately, and word spread like wildfire that a new fly-fishing water was available. Having put in a good stock of big fish, and maintained the stocking density, Mr Welch soon found that he had more anglers than he could handle. There was nothing worse than having to turn anglers away, so he decided to dig out a second lake, again with bulldozers. It lies immediately behind the first lake and is slightly larger and roughly circular. The two lakes total about three and a half acres of fishable water, and both produce fish consistently.

In early 1989 Mr Welch decided that again he had more customers than water, so he purchased some adjacent disused farmland and constructed a third lake, the largest so far, at more than three acres. This is filled by surface run-off water, and opened in April 1989. Mr Welch again set something of a fishery record by completing the excavation of this third lake in a little over five weeks. Once more he used bulldozers, followed by an earth scraper. For anyone excavating a new lake in a clay-based area, this approach must surely be worth considering for its cost-effectiveness.

Much of the area around the fishery formerly belonged to the huge Pallinhurst Estate. This has now been split up, and Mr Welch considers himself fortunate in having been able to secure unused land right next to the first two lakes. The new lake is called Fir Lake and holds rainbows and browns. The success of his initial venture is illustrated by the catch statistics: more than 5000 trout landed in one season alone. Mr Welch maintains a high level of big fish to whet anglers' appetites and is pleased that the water is so clear that they can actually see the fish swimming about in front of them. The fishery records at present stand at: rainbow trout, 17 lb; brown trout, 8 lb 3 oz; and salmon 14 lb. All three records are likely to be broken in the very near future, and may even have been shattered by the time you read this.

To ensure that he is not tied to fish farmers' price increases, Mr Welch is also currently building his own trout farm. This will enable him to keep his prices more competitive by buying the trout in small, then feeding them on himself. He has even managed to rear some himself from eggs, and explains that he rarely goes by the book, since his many years in beef cattle have stood him in good stead as regards animal husbandry. The rainbows and browns grown on by him are all renowned for their good fighting qualities. This is a result of his having taken the advice of a trout farmer to grow his fish on slowly, rather than pump them up on high-protein feed too quickly. The latter approach admittedly produces big trout, but they have a high fat content and are not as well-muscled as trout fed less food over a longer period.

At present Mr Welch has stocked farmed salmon, that is to say, salmon reared artificially and held in pens in a sea loch, of up to 18 lb. Again to cut costs he drives to Scotland to collect them. He splits the costs of purchase and transport with another trout fishery,

Wilf Welch, the owner of Hazel Copse, surveys the bed of the new third lake excavated in the winter of 1988–9.

Anglers brave the winter wind to search out the big rainbow and stillwater salmon stocked into Hazel Copse.

and breaks the journey with an overnight stop. On his first trip he put a galvanized tank on the back of a pick-up, arrived at the salmon fishery, took delivery of his stock, much to the amusement of the fishery boffins who assured him they would not make the journey, and returned home with not one casualty! Mr Welch now works with a lorry and two circular fibre-glass tanks, in which he said the fish travel better. He collects up to 80 salmon at a time, and gets them all back unharmed. Contrary to what others believe, he maintains that salmon travel no worse than rainbow trout.

Mr Welch has also stocked with wild salmon, taken from an estuary. These fish are completely different from the farmed fish, and are continually smashing trout anglers' tackle. While he has a 100 per cent catch rate with the farmed salmon, he may not continue to stock the wild fish as they are simply too strong for trout anglers to land. An interesting fact Mr Welch has discovered is that the salmon can live for up to a year in the lakes, thus giving the fisherman plenty of opportunities to catch them. However, it should be pointed out that many of the regulars at Hazel Copse say that you can see the salmon cruising about but that they can be difficult to take. No salmon caught may be returned to the water.

Stocking takes place two or three times a week, depending on how many fishermen turn up and how many take fish home. Mr Welch offers a sporting ticket for which you pay a nominal sum but must return all the fish you catch. This obviates the need for daily stocking, even though the water is popular. On catch-and-release venues I have heard of four times the usual stocking density per acre being used, as many of the fish simply become too difficult. Hazel Copse seems to have solved that problem, and found a good balance. Mr Welch has actually stocked the two lakes with minnow fry in an effort to provide a natural prey for the big rainbows and salmon. Use a miniature muddler minnow dressing and you could hit one of the big ones.

The sporting ticket mentioned above is so far the most popular, with the record for the fishery being 30 rainbows up to 7 lb caught and returned. To illustrate that this system works, a 10½ lb rainbow was caught just two weeks after being stocked. It was returned to the water and stayed in good condition until it was caught again some five months later. Impressed by its top-level stocking policy, anglers have travelled to Hazel Copse from as far afield as North Wales and Norwich.

Two other interesting points emerge from Mr Welch's efficient

A superb 7½ lb rainbow for Epsom angler Albert Carman. He landed this fish, plus two other rainbows, on a white nymph and floating line.

operation. The first is that he believes the islands in the centre of the lakes are vital to the oxygen content of the water, especially during a long, hot summer. They help to circulate the water in breezy weather, ensuring that he can hold the maximum density of trout in a given area. The second point is that he believes the reason he has a 100 per cent catch rate with the farmed salmon is because they stay in good condition in the water. Apparently, salmon kept in chalk-based water are more likely to pick up fungus than those in a clay-based lake.

The fly life in this rich clay lake is abundant. There are plenty of sedges, varying from flies in a light-brown garb to very large brown ones, particularly good at enticing the bigger browns up on top. The sedges are best during April and early May, but they are also effective right through the summer. The main dry fly is the hawthorn, which has been particularly good, even during a wet and windy winter. The mayfly are not yet abundant. As the lakes are only just maturing, the hatch of this famous late May/early June fly is still somewhat sparse. The hawthorn is voted the most productive fly, possibly due to the heavy woodland surrounding the lakes. There are plenty of damsels, daddy longlegs, water-boatmen and shrimps.

Rather than risk any chemical treatment on the summer weed, Mr Welch likes to drag out any surplus manually. He also believes that if this is done during the early spring, the weed never really grows quite so thick during the summer. He also appreciates the assistance with weed clearing given to him by anglers who stop fishing to help.

SEASONAL TACTICS

Spring

Start with a floating line, and use a long leader. The most popular method is standard nymph fishing, with the fly retrieved about 1 ft beneath the surface. If you want to fish deeper, simply use a heavily weighted nymph such as a Green Beast, Montana, or Mayfly nymph. The Pheasant Tail is also particularly good.

Summer

Now is the time to spend trying the dry fly. Floating line, a long, greased leader and a small Hawthorn or Grey Wulff should get you the occasional fish. Certainly, fish that show no interest around midday will be more active in the last hour of light. Try the very small nymph patterns. Corixa, shrimps, mayflies (even though they have a poor hatch at present) and even the Pheasant Tail tied on a size 12 hook will produce. Buzzers presented in the surface film are good late in the evening, on still days when there is no ripple.

Autumn

Since minnow fry have been stocked, it is certainly worth trying a very small imitative pattern. Fish it deep and jerkily, watching around the margins for any signs of patrolling fish. In September, when there is a good ripple, the daddy longlegs will be active. Try to position yourself so that the fly drifts towards the islands in the first lake. Many of the trout cruise here, hoping they are out of range of many of the anglers.

Winter

Obviously, sinking lines or sink-tips will be the order of the day, but even as late as January 1989 one angler took two rainbows on a dry Mayfly from the first lake. If the weather is mild stay with the dry fly and surface-film nymphs. If it turns cold go deep and fish with fry imitators. Of course, with plenty of other fishermen about you can certainly ring the changes on the depth, speed and pattern they are using. Any fish you want to keep you can have smoked by Loxwood Game (telephone: Loxwood (0403) 752806).

GENERAL INFORMATION

The family are allowed to stay at the fishery, provided they do not disturb the anglers, and there is a barbecue area, and woodland walks through the owner's 22 acres of woodland. Recently a new fishing lodge has been constructed, using storm-damaged wood. This overlooks the lakes and stands at the side of the car park. Mr Welch will take block or club bookings, and operates no rod limit as the stocking density is so high.

The price system at Hazel Copse is as follows:

Full-day ticket: £15.00 (one salmon and three trout, or four trout). Half-day ticket: £10.00 (two trout). The sporting ticket costs £6.00, and all trout caught must be returned unless damaged. If salmon are caught on a half-day ticket or sporting ticket, they are not to be returned, and a full ticket must be paid for. A Thames Water Authority rod licence is required but will be included in the ticket price from April 1990. You can start fishing at 8 AM, and tickets will be collected on the bank. Water depths in the first lake range from 6 ft in the north-east corner down to 12 ft in front of the car park. In the second lake the bank adjoining the first lake is the shallow end, which drops to some 6 ft, while the further end drops to 10 ft. The new lake drops to 14 ft.

Hazel Copse is a good venue to try whether you are an experienced hand or a total beginner. For more information contact: Mr Welch, Hazel Copse Trout Fishery, 7 The Riddens, Tismonds Common, Rudgwick, Sussex. Telephone: Rudgwick (040372) 2878.

HORTON

3 miles from Windsor
4 miles from Slough

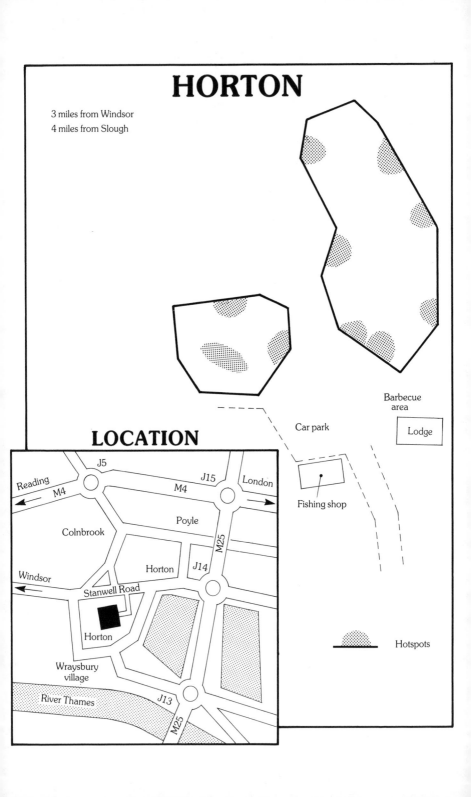

LOCATION

Reading
J5
M4
J15
London
M4
Poyle
Colnbrook
M25
Windsor
Horton
J14
Stanwell Road
Horton
Wraysbury
village
River Thames
J13
M25

Barbecue
area
Car park
Lodge
Fishing shop

Hotspots

HORTON

In the precursor to this book, *A Guide to Small Water Trout Fishing in the South*, also published by Ashford, I mentioned one of the best-cared-for fisheries I have had the pleasure of visiting. Now, for the present book, I have been to a venue that looks even better in terms of facilities. Horton Trout Fishery is located close to the Queen Mother Reservoir, near Slough in Berkshire. The setting is tranquil, with two lakes bordered by mature trees, and the banks carefully manicured. However, there is one annoying drawback. The venue is directly in line with the flight path of Heathrow, the busiest airport in the world, and a morning spent at Horton undoubtedly confirms that fact. When you have a 747 screaming over your head at full take-off power you begin to wonder how the locals can bear it. But, of course, a rising trout is a most welcome distraction, and you do get used to the continual engine noise once you become fully engrossed in the fishing.

Horton is owned by Ready Mixed Concrete, a company well known for supplying coarse anglers with gravel pit fishing that has produced some of the finest ever freshwater catches. Now, Leisure Sport, the divison concerned with fishing, has developed the water into one of the finest trout fisheries I have visited. Much of this fine work must be attributed to Ron Dane, the fishery controller, who runs the complex as though it were his own. The main water, known as Church Lake, is the elder, having been excavated 15–20 years ago for gravel extraction. It is spring-fed and very clear, ideal for insect life and productive sport with trout. After its early years as a coarse fishery (I remember that it was a premier pike water in its day) it was taken over by Kingsmead Trout Farms, with commercially reared trout held in cages. It was not until 1986 that Leisure Sport took control after the trout farm closed, and Ron, then a consultant freelance designer, started the hard work of upgrading everthing to the standard you see today.

For the first year it was run as a season-ticket water, but it was felt that it was unfair to run day tickets in competition with the season-ticket scheme. So it was that Ron decided to run one lake, Church, as an exclusive water for season-ticket holders, and the smaller lake, formed by building a dam across an adjacent lake, as a day-ticket water. So far this system seems to have been a success. The dam is about 40 ft long and sections off Farm Lake as a 10-acre day-ticket water. Here, at the time of writing, no bank fishing is allowed. A strict nature conservancy programme is operated by Ron, who wants the bankside and dam to fully recover before allowing anglers access. There are permanently moored buoys, 15 in all, dotted around the 10 acres, and with 10 large boats for anglers to fish from, it allows plenty of scope to move to other buoys without bothering other anglers. The boats are all brand new, 14 ft, and of fibre-glass clinker design, taking two anglers comfortably.

A season ticket for Church Lake looks very exciting. With an average depth of an amazing 20 ft, the lake gives access to deep water right at the bankside. This allows the angler to see very big rainbows cruising close in, and hopefully a chance to drop a big weighted nymph to them. For the dry-fly specialist this lake has an amazing mayfly hatch down at the copse at the western end, where deep water is right at your feet. There are also plenty of trees, so make sure you cover the area along the bank as well as casting far out. The mayfly have a long season here, sometimes up to six weeks, depending on whether there is a cold spring or not.

As for insect life, the clear water tells its own story. There is an abundance of shrimps, hordes of damselfly, hawthorns, some enormous buzzers, and the normal sedges and olives, which all come because the water is old and therefore well established. The lake is stocked with both brown and rainbow trout, and its depth means that there is little chance of prolific weed growth. Ron is against chemical control of weed, regarding hard labour with a dragline as the best way of extracting it without causing damage to the ecology of the water. The stocking is carried out to a very high standard, with fish Ron purchases from Lambourn and other Berkshire trout farms. Half the stocked fish are between 3 and 3½ lbs, and fish to 20 lb are scheduled for introduction. The peak time for the stocking of big fish is May, so if you are looking for that trophy to hang on the wall, May and June are the months to put the effort in. On Church Lake are kept eight of the 10 large boats, but in fact I found the bank anglers doing just as well as those using boats. I assume that this is because of the access to deep water close in, which improves the bank anglers' chances. Church Lake is limited to 40 anglers per day, and the boats

Anglers' boats scour the small lake for trout. A good ripple produces the best conditions at Horton, and even a strong wind sees the fish taking.

are only bookable by the half day. Fish the banks in the morning and the boat in the afternoon, or vice versa. The stock fish are topped up as trout are caught, and stocking takes place three times a week, mainly with female rainbows and browns of both sexes.

Since Horton was previously a coarse fishery, there is an abundance of coarse fish fry in the margins. These are largely young roach, and so male brown trout are stocked for their aggressive role in helping to control them. There is also a head of big pike, the largest taken by Ron weighing over 34 lb. Thankfully, he believes that some large predators are needed to cull the sickly or weak fish that occur in all waters. The deep water has quite a few gullies and it is here that the big pike patrol. There are also some overwintered fish in superb condition, and hooking one of these will keep your heart pounding for a few minutes.

The day-ticket Farm Lake has a similar ecology to Church Lake and actually backs onto it. This lake has been left to develop wild, so it is a tremendous dry-fly water. Depths average 17 ft, and whereas Church Lake has some bars and gullies, Farm Lake is a regular bowl shape, with an even depth.

Care should be taken when fishing from the stages; a big fish might dive around the platform at the last moment. Here an angler carefully slides the net under a Horton rainbow.

SEASONAL TACTICS

The fishing at Horton is virtually down to individual preference, as trout are caught on everything from dry fly to buzzers, weighted nymphs to lures. A rough seasonal guide to sport would be as follows.

Spring

In cold weather the water temperature will remain most constant down deep. The fry will also be deeper, so use a medium to fast-sink line with a small fry-imitating lure of your choice. Try fast strips early in the morning then slow down as the light gets brighter. The water is very clear, so do not lift off for a recast until you actually see the fly at the end of your leader. If the spring is warm there should be some surface activity, and the bay to the right of the jetty on Church Lake can be good. On Farm Lake, the west bank is productive if you cast in towards the shore to pick up the trout that cruise the margins.

Summer

At this time of year the fishery really looks at its best. The trees and bushes all have foliage and the banks have grown over well. The water temperature is up, and the mayfly on the west-end copse are worth trying around the end of May to mid-June. Floating lines are the order of the day, with either a small lure or large nymph being the most productive patterns. In high summer when the water goes still, fishing will be more difficult, but then this is true of most trout venues. Stay on until the evening and use dry fly, or a team of buzzers in the surface film to pick up the top-water cruisers. Look for cruising big fish in that deep-water margin and present them with a weighted Montana nymph, Mayfly, Damsel or Green Beast. Do not neglect the slow-sink lines if there is a heatwave. Horton's great depth allows the trout to swim deeper, where the cooler thermal layers are, and they are still likely to take a fly fished at that depth, despite the heat. A slow-sink line will enable you to reach them yet still retrieve comparatively slowly.

Autumn

Owing to the abundance of roach fry, the small lures will fish well. Large nymphs fished fast on a slow-sink line will connect you with the rainbows. But remember that those aggressive male browns have been stocked to help control the fry population, and a small lure

The three variations of special Damsel fly which have been tied up for use by Horton regulars. Their catch rate is respectable on other waters as well.

should put you in touch with them. The browns should be in tip-top fighting condition, and those jumbo rainbows will also be looking to a diet of roach to replace the high-protein pellets on which they have been fed. When there is a good ripple on the water is the best time to fish the Daddy Longlegs, and the special Damsel variation tied by Master Fly Tier Paddy Hoey is worth procuring from the tackle shop. It is constructed specially for use at Horton, but anglers using it elsewhere have been extolling its virtues. There is also a special Montana tying that produces fish right through the autumn.

GENERAL INFORMATION

As for amenities for day-ticket fishermen, this venue certainly aims to please. There is adequate parking on hard standings, and invalids are given bankside parking. Separate-sex flush toilets, a tackle shop, food and drink, and picnic tables, complete the picture. Season-ticket holders at Church Lake are even better cared for. They have a members-only lodge and two changing rooms should you arrive from work and need to change into fishing togs. There is a coin-operated coffee and tea machine, a fridge and a small kitchen with a microwave. The lodge is furnished with cane furniture, and the verandah overlooks the main lake.

For both day-ticket and season-ticket holders there is access to a gutting room, something all fisheries should have. That way you avoid a gunky job back at home, and all you do is put the fish straight in the freezer. Just completed is a large stone-slab patio between the two lakes, which is ideal for barbecues and corporate entertainment. A water garden is to be installed, and work is at present under way on a new hospitality building to cater for the exacting needs of corporate groups. The parent company, Thorpe Park, can supply catering at any level, while Horton now offers the bonus of a company day comprising clay-pigeon shooting in the morning and trout fishing in the afternoon. The resident fishing instructor, Tony Pope, and Ron Dane will both be present for these specially organized days. There is no charge for instruction, as a satisfied beginner is likely to turn into a contented regular. Among the big companies who have already booked Horton for these split days are British Airways, Marks and Spencer, Ready Mixed Concrete, and Associated Asphalt.

Six staff now run the venue, with Ron as the manager. The fishery is open from 11 March until November, and fishing times are from 7.30 AM to dusk. There is an abundance of bird life, not just because the water is old and well established, but because Ron has taken the trouble to introduce new species to the water. One section of the property, a rise in the ground, is still used as a conservancy area, and with the lake bordered on three sides by farmland, the wildlife is abundant. Ron has stocked a breeding pair of black swans from the local swan conservancy at Egham. Ducks are there in good numbers as well: tufted, mallard, muscovy, mandarin, Aylesbury, and magpies, plus the usual woodpeckers, kingfishers and reed warblers.

The rules at Horton are fairly standard. Any form of cheating is instantly stamped out, and a telescope is set up on a tripod in the tackle shop, so that offenders are soon caught. Anglers caught using illegal methods will be banned from the fishery, and the management reserves the right to refuse further fishing without explanation. Fishing is by wet fly, dry fly and lures only. Double hooks are not permitted, and no more than three flies may be used at any one time. No more than one rod is to be used at a time by any holder of an individual permit. In the boats, life-jackets must be worn. Boat anglers must tie up to one of the pre-anchored buoys before starting to fish. No trolling is allowed. Do not fish within 20 yards of any bank or jetty, and remove all litter from the boats when you leave. All

Barry Fox from Colchester with the single rainbow he caught from the stagings using a Poly-nymph.

anglers must book in at the fishery office before starting to fish. All trout caught must be killed, and after catching their limit anglers must stop fishing. Fishing and boats must be booked in advance.

The price system is as follows: season rods are split into 10 full, half-day or evening permits, or units. These units are transferable, and guests may be invited on the ticket issued. For the day tickets on Farm Lake the cost is £25.00, including the hire of the boat for a full day, reducing to £20 if two anglers are sharing. The half-day ticket (7 AM–2.15 PM or 2.15 PM until dusk) is available at £15.00 for a single angler in a boat, reducing to £12.50 if the boat is shared. A Thames Water Authority licence is available on site, and flies, leaders, nets, rods and reels can all be bought at the tackle shop. Rod hire is available for those beginners anxious to learn but not yet willing to spend money equipping themselves.

Finally, the family are welcome, and there are picnic tables available. However, they are not allowed onto the banks to disturb other anglers. Horton looks destined to join John Cain's Rockbourne trout fishery as one of the best-run and maintained fisheries in the country, and I feel sure that many others will now have to upgrade their amenities to compete with this new, high-quality venue.

For more information contact: Ron Dane, Fishery Controller, Horton Trout Fishery, Stanwell Road, Horton, Slough, Berkshire SL3 9PE. Telephone: (0753) 684858.

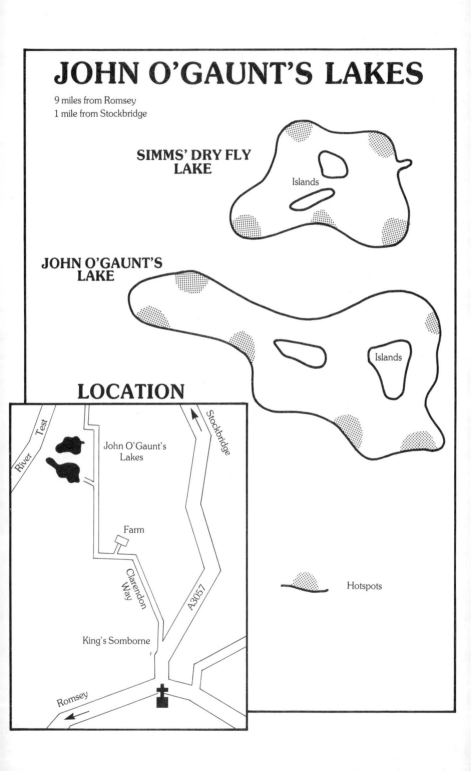

JOHN O'GAUNT'S LAKES

9 miles from Romsey
1 mile from Stockbridge

SIMMS' DRY FLY LAKE

Islands

JOHN O'GAUNT'S LAKE

Islands

LOCATION

River Test

John O'Gaunt's Lakes

Stockbridge

Farm

Clarendon Way

A3057

King's Somborne

Romsey

Hotspots

JOHN O' GAUNT'S LAKES

River anglers have long regarded stillwater anglers as something less than the 'real thing', putting them in the 'throw-it-out-and-pull-it-back' category. This view is to a large extent true of anglers on many stillwaters, and is borne out by the huge popularity and success of lure fishing over the last decade. While many anglers look to a fishery to produce fish of immense size, to order, it was recently my pleasure to spend a day at a fishery that puts the emphasis on quality of presentation rather than on a limit bag of stew-pond monsters.

Of course, every angler must by now appreciate that all trout in put-and-take fisheries are fed stock fish, whether they are 1 lb or 20 lb. Credibility is difficult to sustain in a situation where the fish are known not to be wild. However, the first of John O' Gaunt's two lakes, a mere five and a half acres of sparkling Hampshire splendour, has that quality of a true chalkstream, but in a stillwater. It is adjacent to what is possibly the most famous river trouting in the world, namely that of the Houghton stretch of the River Test, so the lake is steeped in history by association. I had visited the lake many years ago when it was run for 10 years by Mike Simms, yet even then it was a secret except to local anglers. The lake was dug about 14 years ago for the extraction of gravel, but after a few years natural springs were hit and the lake was formed through flooding – hardly surprising when you see the majestic Test running alongside it, where access to the fishing is only via 'dead men's shoes'.

Now the fishery is run by one Jack Sheppard, who at the tender age of 23 became the youngest RSM ever in the British Army. He had joined the Royal Horse Artillery at 16, and finished as a Captain. Given his familiarity with discipline, it is easy to see how he attaches that same importance to his trout fishing. He learnt the art of true chalkstream fishing from the master of the river, Frank Sawyer. He learnt the upstream nymph technique from Frank, and salmon fishing from Reg Righyni. As well as managing John O' Gaunt's Lakes, Jack runs the Chalkstream School of Flyfishing from Alresford, looking after some half a million pounds' worth of fishing on the rivers Dun, Arle and Itchen.

In just an hour spent chatting with Jack I learnt more about river trout fishing than I have read in a number of years. It is the attraction of chalkstream fishing that Jack tries to retain within the gin-clear water of this venue. When I arrived he was telling everyone to use a floating line and Green Nymph retrieved slowly across the surface. Usually you get few tips from fishery managers, and I was pleased to see him taking such an interest in teaching beginners to catch trout with the delicate approach and thoughtful cast. I must confess, though, to some embarrassment over my double-hauling casts that sent the line out near the island, even though I did pick up my limit within the hour, and yes . . . all on a Green Nymph!

This fishery is an interesting piece of water to fish, given the exceptional clarity and correct presentation. Jack actually saw a take on my line before I felt it, and that when he was standing on the other side of the lake! Although the lake holds a residue of nice browns, the main stocking is undertaken weekly with rainbows of 1¾–6 lb, and all in very presentable condition. Depths range from viewable shallows right down to 15 ft where the springs are, and since these are possibly the same springs that feed the Test there is a constant temperature all the year round, at spring level, of 53–54° F. For this reason the fish are spread around, so I advise spending an hour in one spot, then moving round to another, searching out new fish. Your first indication is likely to be visual as a fly disappears from the surface film. Both rainbows and browns can top 6 lb here, so beware of that last-minute crash-take.

In the 1989 season 1,189 rods took 3,054 fish for a 2.57 fish-per-rod average. Large trout are not what Jack Sheppard's fishery aims at. Its rainbow record stands at 4¾ lb, while the brown trout record is 4 lb 2 oz. Now, a second lake of two and a half acres and holding 90 million gallons of water has been added, immediately adjacent to the first, and has been designated as dry-fly only. Jack has the satisfaction of seeing mayfly from the nearby Test going straight onto the new lake, an interesting occurrence that could cast new light on the mayfly cycle. Until now it was thought that it took two years from the mayfly spinner stage to the new mayfly hatch, but Jack believes this lake is now the first water to see mayfly lay eggs and go on to provide a hatch the following year. The dry-fly lake was opened in the spring

Quality of environment and quality of fish are the two selling points of Jack Sheppard's John O' Gaunt's fishery. The rainbows are not monsters, but at 3 and 4 lb provide exciting sport in peaceful surroundings.

of 1988, finished in mid-April, and settled down remarkably quickly.

The six-month cycle of insect life has already established itself, with buzzers being particularly abundant. Add the wealth of snails and shrimp, and the fly fisherman has plenty of choice both as to depths to fish and patterns to use. Doubtless the weed will soon start to flourish, adding even more insect life to what is already a prolfiic water. The irony is that Jack paid £1000 for chemical treatment of the main lake to keep weed down, and now needs more weed in the new lake! Such are the problems facing the modern fishery owner. The new lake has been landscaped with trees and shrubs, making John O' Gaunt's a very attractive venue indeed. Stock is obtained from Mick Lunn at the famed Houghton club, quality rather than size being the aim.

SEASONAL TACTICS

Spring

With a constant water temperature courtesy of the spring water, there is little need on this fishery for fast or even medium-sink lines. A slow-sink line might be useful in cold weather, but an intermediate will suit conditions better. The rainbows are likely to be swimming shallower than the browns, so if using a slow-sink line, stick to snail or shrimp. If rainbows are the quarry, any of the standard nymphs will produce: Gold Ribbed Hare's Ear, Montana, Mayfly or Damsel. As soon as the water warms up try unweighted nymphs and a floating line, matching any hatch that occurs in late April.

Summer

Surface-film fishing with buzzers, or dry fly on the new lake, should be looked into, but check first with Jack, who has an intimate knowledge of entomology. He can advise on patterns to correspond exactly with any hatching insects. There will be plenty of iron blue dun, dark olives and sedge, plus of course the mayfly spinners from the river, even if a new hatch does not occur on the dry-fly lake. Stick with either floating line or intermediates, but make sure you try traditional wet-fly patterns such as Peter Ross, Butcher and Wickham's Fancy. When selecting nymphs, give priority to Demoiselle, Frank Sawyer's Killer Bug, Pheasant Tail nymphs and Montana.

Autumn

The fishing is virtually the same as in summer. Both lakes are sheltered, and unless there is a specific hatch of anything I advise a very slow-sink line towards September, when things slow down a bit. Stick to traditional wet-fly patterns. No large leaded lures are allowed, nor are they needed. Check with Jack Sheppard first if you are unsure about any autumn patterns.

GENERAL INFORMATION

The facilities and rules are fairly standard. In contrast to many fishery owners, Jack welcomes all the family, even dogs, provided they are kept under strict control. There is adequate parking, toilets, a picnic area and a barbecue area. The fishery opens on 1 February and closes on 31 October. Fishing times are from 9 AM to dusk, but stay on well into the evening in high summer as the rise can be quite exciting. Payment for the permit implies acceptance of the fishery's rules, which are basically as follows. A Southern Water Authority licence is required before fishing. Fly fishing only is allowed, with a single hook no larger than a Partridge No. 8. The overall length limit is 1 in. Fast-sink, lead-core and shooting-head lines are banned. Fishing must cease when the limit on the ticket has been reached. Children under 14 are not allowed unless accompanied by an adult. Wading is not allowed. All fish caught should be recorded, including nil returns.

Now, with eight acres of gin-clear chalkstream water available, the discerning trout angler has a venue where the emphasis is on tradition rather than quantity and size. Ticket prices are as follows:

Full-day ticket: £18.50 (four-fish limit).
Half-day ticket (9 AM–2 PM or 2 PM until dusk): £12.00 (two-fish limit).
Season ticket: details on application.

Block bookings for either club or corporate days are welcome, with special rates available on application. For more information contact: Jack Sheppard, John O' Gaunt's Lakes, Clarendon Way, Cowgrove Hill, King's Somborne, Hampshire SO51 7TB. Telephone: Romsey (0794) 388130; after hours: (0962) 734864.

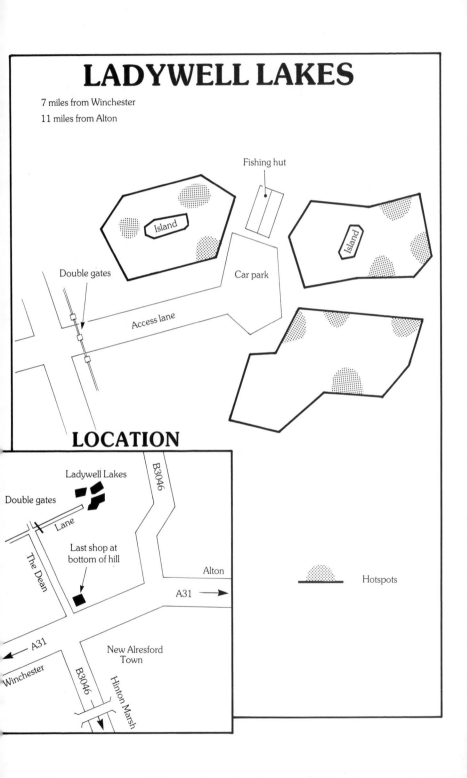

LADYWELL LAKES

7 miles from Winchester

11 miles from Alton

Fishing hut

Island

Island

Double gates

Car park

Access lane

LOCATION

Ladywell Lakes

B3046

Double gates

Lane

Last shop at
bottom of hill

Alton

A31 →

The Dean

← A31

Winchester

New Alresford
Town

B3046

Hinton Marsh

Hotspots

LADYWELL LAKES

Finding a trout fishery in the heart of historic southern England makes the fishing all the more pleasurable. South-west of Alton in Hampshire are Ladywell Lakes. Virtually in the town of New Alresford, the lakes are tucked away down a side turning, and perfectly secluded. For those interested in history, Alton grew quietly prosperous from brewing and the manufacture of woollen cloth. A busy market town, it stands at the top of the hills I would describe as the start of the Meon valley. New Alresford itself is regarded by many as one of the last true villages, and during the medieval period grew to be one of the ten greatest wool towns in the country. The aptly named Broad Street leads downhill to Old Alresford, and at the north-west end of the village is the large and picturesque parish pond. By turning into Station Road you can visit the Mid Hants Railway.

All this area is prime river-trouting country. You have the tiny Arle, the famous Itchen and not far away the miniature Meon. The Tichborne area is also good, but it must be said that most of the stream trouting is tied up privately, with little or no chance of access. Tichborne village has a delightful collection of thatched sixteenth and seventeenth-century houses, together with a tiny church and a nineteenth-century manor house.

Ladywell Lakes are quite small and attract mainly local trout anglers. They were created some 12 years ago by excavation of former watercress beds. The water is so pure that watercress beds abound in this area, and if the water is pure then the trout will thrive in it. There are also chalk hills nearby that filter any pollutants, keeping the water fresh and clear. The three lakes total just under three acres, and their area will not be expanded as the property is bounded by houses and a stream.

Ladywell was run as a regular trout fishery offering both day and season tickets, and was originally in the garden of the former owner. It was taken over in 1987 by Mr Ng, who confesses to not being a trout fisherman, but who purchased the land purely because it came with planning permission, and he has always wanted a house near water! Given the position of the foundations of the house, it will almost be a case of fishing out of the lounge window! Since he originates from Hong Kong, perhaps this will not seem too unfamiliar to Mr Ng. With the recent increase in the cost of trout from fish farmers and rising costs of feed, Mr Ng was fortunate to purchase some adjacent land over the stream and has been excavating with a digger to form more stock ponds. That way he can buy the trout in smaller and feed them on at his own rate, so keeping his day-ticket prices competitive.

Once the new stock ponds are established, they will hold up to 3000 trout and will be used to provide new stock as fish are taken by anglers. It is therefore important for anglers to fill in any catch returns so as to enable the management to restock at the proper density. Stocking is done on a daily basis.

The three lakes are fed both by the tiny Arle and underground springs coming from a header pond up in Alresford. These lakes are on the whole quite shallow and often suffer from weed. Shallow depths, coupled with pure chalkstream water, allow strong light penetration, which in turn boosts weed growth. Here, this is mainly blanket weed, which puts in an early appearance in spring, blooms in hot weather and pops to the surface in brown mats. Mr Ng has treated the weed with chemicals, which minimizes growth; but much still has to be dragged out by hand. This cannot be done in spring as the mats are not thick enough on the surface. In summer, when a breeze has pushed the weed to one end of the lake, it is heavier but more easily removed. This procedure can put a slight green tinge in the water, but the water's clarity is such that on a sunny day you still have the chance to spot your trout.

APPROACH AND TACKLE

The three lakes are known as Fuller's, Miller's and Tanner's. Fuller's is the largest, ranging from 3 ft right down to 18 ft in the corner nearest the fishing hut. The shallow end is by the gates where you enter the fishery. There is a small island in the centre designated as a wildfowl refuge. On Fuller's, the area immediately in front of the fishing hut and slightly to the right is a good place to try. This is right next to the car park, so try to watch your back cast. I recently saw an angler clip the cars on his back cast, and he was using a heavy weighted nymph at that! Tanner's is located immediately behind the

Medstead fly fisherman, John Thornton, used fast-sinking line, a 5 lb leader and a small yellow lure to take this superb 5½ lb Ladywell rainbow. He has landed one of 8 lb previously, and rates the fishery highly.

fishing hut and for some reason does not seem to attract so much attention from the anglers. This lake is used for brown trout fishing only, and since they soon begin to wise up after being pricked and lost, they demand a little more care in approach and presentation. The depth in Tanner's drops to around 10 ft in the centre, and this could well be where some of those larger browns are. The fish in this lake range from 2 lb up to 6 lb, although there are thought to be one or two larger browns yet to come out.

Immediately adjacent to this lake is Miller's, stocked, like Fuller's, with rainbows only, ranging from 2 lb up to 10 lb. This is where Mr Ng has had his house built. Most fishermen would certainly be envious as it is built right into the bank. There is a slight tinge of green near the house where the water has coloured owing to the chalk foundations. Eventually, though, the water should go gin-clear, and allow good visual spotting of trout. There are also several big carp in the lakes, running to over 25 lb, put in by the previous owner in order to keep the weed down. The centre of Miller's is the same depth as Tanner's, 10 ft, and slow-sink lines are generally best.

As for insect life, a system of small lakes being fed by such pure water is bound to have plenty. There are lots of mayfly, which can start as early as mid-May and run on into mid-June. In 1988 the

Working a line for one of the bigger browns in the centre lake at Ladywell.

mayfly hatch ran right to the end of June, a phenomenon I noticed at several other trout venues that year. Owing to the prolific weed growth at Ladywell there is an abundance of damselfly, which fish particularly well when a breeze is blowing. Fishermen interested in scouring the depths for those larger browns in Tanner's lake should try shrimps in an orange or black dressing. If you fish a weighted shrimp, use a slow-sink line, or, with an unweighted shrimp, use a fast-sink line. There are corixa, snails and lots of tadpoles, particularly in the latter part of April. For surface fishing you can imitate sedges, olives, mayfly and daddy longlegs. The fishery records at the time of writing stand at 13 lb for rainbow trout and 7 lb for brown. The record rainbow was landed by the former fishery bailiff, George Cook, on a Montana Nymph, sinking line and a 6 lb leader. The brown fell to Ernie Smith of London, who was using a wiggletail lure.

SEASONAL TACTICS

Spring

The waters are quite deep and any weed is unlikely to have grown very much. Therefore try a slow-sink line, searching out the deeper corners of Fuller's with a small lure. Remember, though, that no large lures of more than 1 in overall length are allowed. Appetiser and Viva are the best patterns. Towards the middle of April an increase in light and warmth will bring on the weed and you may find you have to start your retrieve a little earlier in order to bring the fly up over the weedbeds. Use standard wet-fly patterns or try a large Killer Bug or Aggravator, tweaked along. This is certainly a good method on Miller's. Leader tippets will have to drop from about 6 lb when you are sunk-line fishing to 4 lb if you intend to fish buzzers in the surface film.

Summer

There may be quite a bit of blanket weed popping up on the surface and drifting into a corner of the lakes, where it forms a brown mat. The trout will often lie beneath this, and you can catch them by bringing your fly back along the edge of the weed. If there is no wind to drift the weed into mats, you can often spot fish lying beneath single portions of blanket weed. Drop a weighted nymph to them, then tweak it away and you may well get a confident response. The Mayfly can be fished dry on the surface, and Fuller's Lake is good in

Casting a line in the third lake for rainbows. The fishery is compact but holds some fine fish.

this respect, particularly if you cast towards the edge of the island. In July, when temperatures may be at their peak, try fishing with a green or orange buzzer in the surface film, using a leader as light as perhaps 3 lb, and a floating line. The lakes are very small, so you may prefer to keep well away from the fish you are casting to.

Autumn

These lakes contain very few fry, so there is little point in going back to small lures. After a season of seeing anglers' lines, any really large fish may be out around the edges of the island in Fuller's. Stick to a floating line, but cast a weighted nymph close to the edge of the island and retrieve it slowly. As for the other two lakes, their clear water may give you a chance of spotting a bigger trout visually and presenting a weighted nymph to him. Do not forget that the back end of September can be good for fishing the Daddy Longlegs on the surface, which is best done when a good south-westerly wind has been blowing. Also, very small dry flies such as the Black Gnat work well, but make sure that you put a good distance between yourself and the fish before casting. The lakes are very small and you must avoid spooking the fish.

Finally, it seems that in 1990 there will be the chance to lure fish in the traditional way, thousands of roach and carp fry having now established themselves.

GENERAL INFORMATION

The season at Ladywell starts on Open Day, which is 1 April, and runs to the end of September. This may be extended as Mr Ng gets more established. Fishing times are from 9 AM until half an hour before sunset. All the fish come from Dave Reilly's Itchen Valley Trout Farm, famous for its top-quality fish. All the anglers I spoke to were satisfied with both the fighting and culinary qualities of these fish.

The prices are as follows:

Day ticket: £20.00 (four-fish limit: four rainbows or two rainbows and two browns).
Half-day ticket (9 AM to 3 PM, or 3 PM until half an hour before sunset): £12.00 (two-fish limit).

At present no evening tickets are available. As for season-ticket prices, a full season, which consists of 26 sessions, receives a 10 per cent discount on the daily price, while a half-day season of 13 sessions also offers a 10 per cent reduction. The facilities include a car park, a toilet, and a fishing hut, and Mr Ng hopes to sell flies and leaders. No tackle is available for hire, and barbecues are not allowed. Families are welcome for picnics, but must keep away from the edge of the lakes. The three lakes take a maximum of 10 anglers, but can be taken over either for a corporate day or for a club booking. Advance booking is required; there are no tickets generally available to casual visitors.

For more information contact: Mr Ng, Ladywell Trout Lakes, The Dean, Alresford, Hampshire. Telephone: (03727) 20128.

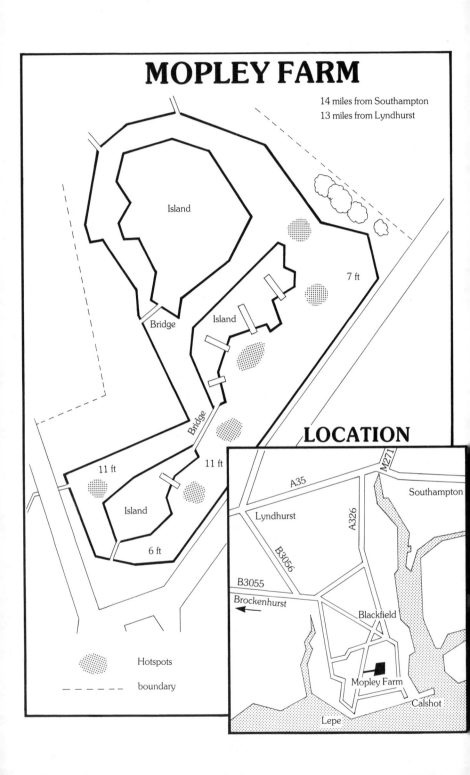

MOPLEY FARM

If ever the expression 'small is beautiful' can be applied to a fishery, it could be tagged onto Mopley Farm. The first time I saw this tiny water I could scarcely believe it. Small it is, but the longer you stay there the more relaxed you become, and tiny bays suddenly look very fishy indeed. This is certainly not a par-for-the-course fishery, as it has the added benefit of an area that is sectioned off for any-method trout fishing. The purists will undoubtedly react with alarm, but this is something that I think should be done on a far wider scale, certainly on the larger open reservoirs.

Brian Tillman runs the fishery, which he took over in 1984, and also operates a countryside activity centre. Situated in the middle of the Manor of Cadland, and bounded by Southampton Water and the Solent, the pond has a setting that is perfect for sheltered fishing. It is located just 15 miles from Southampton, adjacent to the New Forest, and is within easy reach of London by car: about 1½ hours on the M3. British Rail's Intercity Service serves Southampton. Bed and breakfast can be arranged with Brian.

Mopley Farm House, overlooking the fishery, is a nineteenth-century red-brick building, the history of which is a little obscure. The bricks came from the now-disused kiln at nearby Langley. Along with a mill at nearby Little Stanswood, Langley was first mentioned in the Domesday Book of 1086. The farmhouse was probably built on the site of a dwelling used by the mill keeper, for Mopley Pond was one of a series of ponds used to supply water to the mill at Little Stanswood. The valley running from Mopley via Little Stanswood down to the sea at Stanswood Bay is now part of the North Solent Nature Reserve.

The Manor of Cadland and the surrounding countryside is laced with public footpaths, many of which pass through conifer planta-tions, over open areas and alongside the saltings of Southampton Water. The area is rich in wildlife and the careful observer may occasionally see deer, Dartford warblers, kingfishers, herons and a wide variety of wading and sea birds. One afternoon in October

1982, 47 species were reported to have been seen within a 2-mile radius of Mopley Farm. Plenty to occupy the trout fisherman interested in the countryside as well as the water at his feet!

When Brian took over the running of the venue, the tiny pond was even smaller and used as a coarse fishery for beginners. The Estate has been owned by the Drummonds since 1772, and in 1983, as part of a public relations scheme, was dredged by Ready Mixed Concrete, with financial help from the Estate. So many tiny mill-ponds fall into disrepair, and quickly become silted up, giving a foothold to waterside plants, bushes and trees that eventually over-grow the place. This in turn acts as a barrier for the silt that builds up around the root systems. Soon there is little water remaining – just an overgrown swamp area. Such was the case at this water, where RMC's dredging operation removed over 9 ft of silt. The machinery was also used to cut new channels around the overgrown islands, to enlarge the fishable area. Consequently there is now some move-ment around these islands, which maintains the oxygen content of the water and provides nooks and crannies for the trout to hole up in.

APPROACH AND TACKLE

The water is L-shaped, with the main dam wall being the deepest area, offering depths from about 11 ft near the monk's hatch overflow, to 7 ft at each end. This is the area designated for fly fishing, and holds a good number of rainbows and browns. Contrary to popular opinion, the any-method section appears to do no harm to the trout stocks. No keepnets are allowed, so the fish must be unhooked and returned alive. This sets up a learning process in the trout's memory that makes it more of a capture when it is taken on the fly. The bait that wreaks devastation on new stocks is sweetcorn. Rainbows go wild for it, but success here actually leads them to move out of the any-method area and into the long straight, where fly fishing is allowed. Therefore the water creates its own balance as to distribution of the fish. Early stock fish will fall to the any-method anglers, while the wiser and harder-fighting fish will move on to an insect and fry diet.

While the rainbows range far and wide through the open water, the browns tend to patrol very close to the bank, especially along the dam area. In summer the water will clear and you can spot fish individually, although browns are not the easiest fish to take visually.

They do, however, respond very well to dry fly in June, around the narrow necks of the islands and near the bridges opposite the farmhouse. This area is always very still and doubtless affords a good opportunity for any hatching insects. With all the trees in the valley, there will also be the bonus of terrestrial fall-ins to perk up any browsing brownie.

The outlet from the monk's hatch occasionally has a run of sea trout. Brian hopes to widen this overspill stream without harming the surrounding landscape, and intends putting in holding pools and creating a small brown trout fishery. Two springs feed the main pond, and depths generally remain good even through a hot summer. If you intend to pursue these brown trout, note that the smaller dry-fly patterns produce most consistently. There are some overwintered fish and they take only miniature dry mayfly, which you may have to tie yourself, or the Black Gnat.

SEASONAL TACTICS

Spring

This water is sheltered, so there is every chance that there will be some surface activity. It depends largely on how cool the breeze is, so certainly start with a slow-sink line if you see no fish moving, as they may not be far down. Effective patterns are Whisky Fly and Jersey Herd which, being orange, have good visibility in slightly coloured water. The Black Aggravator is also good. Towards late spring, during midday and evening, switch to buzzer fishing. Orange, red or black are the taking colours. If the spring is very cold, try fishing off the dam close to the bank, casting laterally rather than straight out. Use a stick fly, a shrimp or a bright lure in the smaller patterns, and fish it in sharp tweaks rather than long pulls.

Summer

The best of the brown trout may come to the dry-fly man who sits back from the bank in the corner by the farmhouse and watches for a rising fish. Small dry flies will get most takes, but present them carefully. This is a small water, and any fish you spook may be the only one in that area. Try also the slow-sink line with corixa, or a large Gold Ribbed Hare's Ear, but fished in long, slow pulls. There is no need to strip in fast – you want to scare any fish as little as possible. Leader strength can be as low as 3 lb, but watch for the

The tiny water of Mopley Farm is deceptive. There are big trout there, but they need careful presentation. Here David Glaister fishes deep water for a big rainbow.

bigger fish. Small hook sizes also dictate that you should use care when playing any fish.

Autumn

This is the time of year to try a medium-sink line, a greased leader and a small lure inched over the bottom close to the margins. There is a large head of wild brown trout fry, and the bigger trout eat these as avidly as they do the coarse fish fry. I have not yet heard of a fly dressing that resembles a trout fry, so you will have to look through your fly wallet and let your imagination run riot! For surface fishing, the Daddy Longlegs will be favourite, especially on damp, muggy evenings towards the back end of September. Standard nymph fishing will still connect with the smaller rainbows, but having been caught and returned by the any-method anglers, the bigger fish will need a more subtle approach. Keep your leaders to 6 lb when fishing a sinking line.

GENERAL INFORMATION

The trout season at Mopley Pond runs from 1 March to 30 September, and the rules are fairly basic. No large lead-headed lures are allowed, and frankly you do not need them. Only one fly is to be used at a time, and droppers are banned. All fish caught must be recorded for the purpose of keeping a log book to allow restocking. Anglers, having caught their bag limit, must record their catch. If the ticket time permits, they may continue to fish on barbless hooks, returning the trout to the water or paying for any extra trout taken. Permits are not transferable. Rod sharing is permitted, but only one rod may be used by one person at any one time, and the fish limit is that of the guest and ticket holder combined. The fly fisherman can go anywhere on the lake, including the any-method area, but any-method anglers must stick to the designated area. The use of boats and wading are not permitted.

Day-ticket fishing times are 9 AM to sunset. Half-day tickets run from 9 AM to 2.30 PM or 2.30 PM to sunset. Evening tickets run from 5.30 PM to sunset. All fishermen must pay, and be booked in, before starting to fish. All rods fishing alongside the public footpath must respect the right of way of pedestrians. All fishermen must be in possession of a priest and landing net. There is a car park, tea and coffee can be arranged, and there is a new tackle shop where you can purchase flies, nets, leaders, etc. Rod hire, for either a beginner

A fine catch of rainbows for David Glaister. He used both the Montana nymph and a tadpole on a sink-tip line, searching out the gullies and banks for fish. His largest to date weighed 7 lb 14 oz.

or those who forget their tackle, is just £2.30 a day. This would be an ideal water for group or club booking, so I advise you to ask Brian if he will offer discount for mid-week bulk deals.

For the family, the situation is ideal. You have pleasant wooded walks, and the saltings of Southampton Water. About 5 miles away is Beaulieu, with Lord Montagu's National Motor Museum. Buckler's Hard is a pretty village 3 miles downstream from Beaulieu river, and a maritime museum commemorates the naval shipyard that flourished there in the eighteenth century. Nelson's warship *Agamemnon* was built here. The nearby Exbury Gardens are world renowned and are best seen during May and June, which coincides with the best dry-fly fishing, so the family can leave you in peace!

Longdown is the home of the New Forest Butterfly Farm, which has a picnic area and an adventure playground, and is about 8 miles from the fishery. Finally, the country park at Lepe offers walking, birdwatching or windsurfing, about 2 miles away. Nearby Calshot is also good for walking.

Ticket prices are as follows:

Day ticket: £17.25 (four-fish limit).
Half-day ticket; £10.35 (two-fish limit).
Evening ticket: £6.90 (one-fish limit).
Season ticket (31 named days): £392.15.
Company day/club/block booking: ask for details.

For more information contact: Brian Tillman, Mopley Farm Fishery, Mopley Road, Blackfield, Southampton SO4 IYH. Telephone: Fawley (0703) 891616.

NYTHE LAKES

8 miles from Winchester
10 miles from Alton

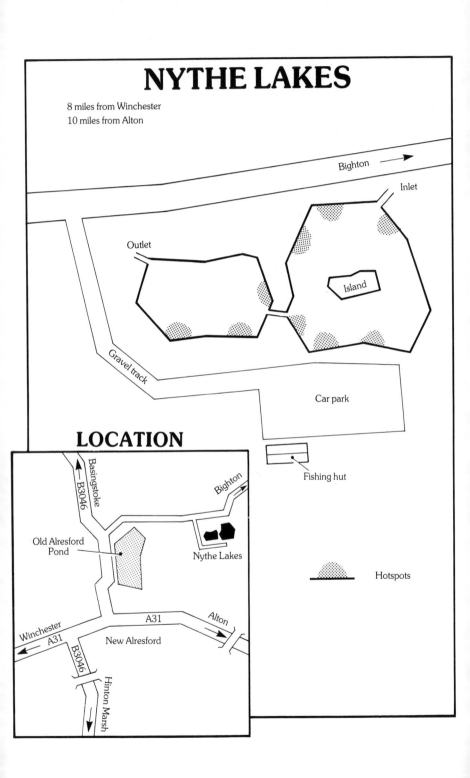

Bighton →

Inlet

Outlet

Island

Gravel track

Car park

LOCATION

B3046 Basingstoke

Bighton →

Old Alresford Pond

Nythe Lakes

Fishing hut

Winchester

← A31

B3046

A31

New Alresford

Alton →

Hinton Marsh

Hotspots

NYTHE LAKES

If there is one venue that has quietly led the field with catches of very big trout, it must be Hampshire's Nythe Lakes. This fishery has probably produced, for its size, more double-figure fish than any other. Just two lakes, totalling a miniscule one and a quarter acres, are on offer to the fly fisherman and, with a restricted rod limit, the venue is so productive that to get a weekend you may have to book a year in advance! Located near Bighton, Nythe Lakes are set in one of the most popular areas for country driving. The Mid Hants Railway, or the 'Watercress Line', as it has come to be known, is nearby, and worth visiting. Also close by is Alresford, with its Broad Street, said to be the finest example of a wide village street in Hampshire. The village is an ideal base for anybody trouting for a few days in the area.

The main reason for the huge fish-per-rod ratio at Nythe Lakes is that the fishery is owned and run by Dave Reilly. Dave's name has been linked to the very best of trout farming, and his stock is regarded by many as simply the best available in Britain. I visit many trout fisheries and I have yet to receive a single complaint about the quality of Dave's stock. Running Itchen Valley Trout Farm, below Alresford, means that Dave can give clients fishing his water the benefit of his expertise as a trout farmer. Nowhere in the country offers such intensive stocking, yet it still remains for you, the angler, to winkle out the fish.

Dave has been in the fish-farming business for 20 years, and his operation produces millions of trout fry and thousands of stock fish each year. He supplies dozens of other trout fisheries, specializing in producing sporting fish rather than fish for the restaurant trade. He even supplies other trout farms, and stocks water all over the country, from tiny streams and rivers such as the Wylye, Dever, Test, Itchen and Meon, through the whole range of put-and-take fisheries, up to huge man-made reservoirs such as Rutland Water and Queen Mother Reservoir. Even the tiny New Forest stream of Brockenhurst

A big trout on, and the angler strains to pressure the fish into the net.

has had some of Dave's stock fish. Many of his early customers have remained loyal to him, some for as long as eighteen years.

As for intensive feeding, Dave aims to produce a lot of good-quality, regular-size trout rather than jumbo trout. Even so, he has reared rainbows to over 20 lb, and sold them at weights up to 18¾ lb. Browns also have been pushed to over 9 lb, and Dave hopes to sell out each year with these, for they are always in demand. He only keeps fish from the egg stage for three years, and can produce a near 20-pounder in around four years. Dave was also one of the first to cross-breed the Tiger and Cheetah hybrids, but as they did not appeal to his regular customers he sold his stock of Brook trout to the late Sam Holland, of Avington fame, who broke several British records with this species.

The two lakes that form the fishery are located down a gravel track, and can just be seen from the road, behind some farm buildings. You could easily miss the track, so drive carefully. The lakes were dug as a trout fishery many years ago, and are now stable and rich in feed. They are small, but very deep, which allows a good holding of fish per acre. The smaller lake drops to 14 ft, while the larger water has a more gradual depth change from about 6 ft down to 16 ft. The weed life is abundant, and is chemically treated to

Into the net slides a good Nythe rainbow. The art lies in finding the small areas between the weedbeds where the fish feed.

Unhooking a big Nythe rainbow. The fishery quietly produces some of the best quality trout in the country.

minimize growth. The water crowfoot is very lush, as is mare's tail, ranunculus and other species associated with chalk streams. These create a haven for all manner of insect life, especially snails and shrimps, on both of which many of the fish feed.

APPROACH AND TACKLE

There is no mayfly hatch on this water. This is due, Dave assures me, to the fact that it is so close to the headwaters of the river Arle. Mayfly like mud, and the headwaters are in fact too clean to support them. This is possibly the only fishery I know where you can run through the entire season using one or two techniques – all due to the fact that the water is very clear, weedy and deep. This is prime territory for the individual stalking of big rainbows: fish in excess of 4 lb and up to and beyond the double-figure mark. You need no fast-sink lines here, because although the water is very deep, both lakes will have abundant weed growth that pushes up towards the surface, narrowing down the area in which you will find trout. Naturally, they must get in among any dense weed to take the rich feed of nymphs, shrimps and snails, but the larger fish like to patrol an area of clear water immediately adjacent to the weed. It is the fly fisherman who seeks out these deep, clear areas who will score best.

The art of stalking fish individually has been well documented elsewhere, but basically you should use either a floating or a slow-sink line, a long leader of around 10 ft or more, and a weighted nymph. Shop-bought nymphs rarely carry enough lead in the dressing, so you would be well advised to tie your own. When you spot a trout, cast well ahead of him to avoid spooking him. At Nythe this is all the more important since the water is gin-clear, and invariably any trout will be swimming a lot deeper than it appears to be. While small rainbows of a couple of pounds will rush over and inhale a fly with gusto, bigger fish of over 6 lb need the nymph right in front of their noses, and seldom move more than a foot off course.

If the trout does not speed up and engulf the nymph, give a few tweaks to impart life to the dressing, making the hackles twitch. Do not chase after the fish, thrashing the water to a foam. Simply wait for him to come round again on his patrolling route, and give him another chance. If he shows no interest in three casts, change the pattern completely, going from bright to dull or vice versa. Some anglers at Nythe like to use a slow-sink line since this allows you to fish the deep holes further down simply by leaving more time for the fly to sink. It also allows you to fish the fly laterally through the water, rather than at an inclined angle, as you do when using a floating line.

This venue has a limit of just six anglers per day, which means that advance booking is required. No tickets are available on the bank. The fishery rules are fairly standard. No lures, lead-headed or otherwise, are allowed, nor are they needed. The maximum hook size is 10, with a maximum dressing length of 1 in. No teams of flies are allowed. All fish caught must be recorded. You will need a good pair of polarizing sunglasses and a wide-peaked hat to help you spot the fish. But even on a day when the breeze has put a ripple on the surface, you can distinguish enough to see where the weedbeds are. Fish the deep holes to the side of them and you will have as good a chance as anyone. At present the fishery record for rainbow trout is 17 lb 12 oz, but this is always open to challenge, for some big fish cruise these clear waters. The brown trout record is also substantial at 8 lb 10 oz. The averages for 1988 were three fish per rod and 3 lb per fish, which, taken over a whole season, are very good figures indeed.

One of the best things about Nythe is that it is small enough to be booked during the week by a club or even a group of friends. It can be much more fun to fish in a group, and you find the experienced anglers showing the beginners what to do for the best results. If you take one of these small private parties, Dave will allow you to have a barbecue.

SEASONAL TACTICS

Spring, Summer, and Autumn

Fish a floating line with small dry flies, right down to a Black Gnat in the warm evenings when you see fish moving on the top. This approach can also be good first thing in the morning, when the rainbows are swimming nearer the surface. After the first hour they will go down, and you can either go stalking with floating line and weighted nymph, or fish the deeper holes by 'feel', using a slow-sink line. For the sub-surface work stay with the usual nymphs, but make sure they have extra lead in the dressing. Use Montana, Damsel, Gold Ribbed Hare's Ear, Large Pheasant Tail, Green Shrimp and even the Mayfly, despite there being no hatch of this insect.

GENERAL INFORMATION

The fishery is open from 25 March until 31 October, and offers good rainbow and brown trout throughout this period. Prices are as follows:

Day ticket: £25.00 (four-fish limit).
Half-day ticket: £15.00 (two-fish limit). Half-day tickets are available on the day by advance booking. No tackle is available for sale or hire, so make sure that you take all you need. There is no instruction. The fishery has a car park, a toilet and a fishing hut with scales.

For more information contact: Dave Reilly, Nythe Trout Lakes, Itchen Valley Trout Farm, New Alresford, Hampshire. Telephone: (0962) 734489.

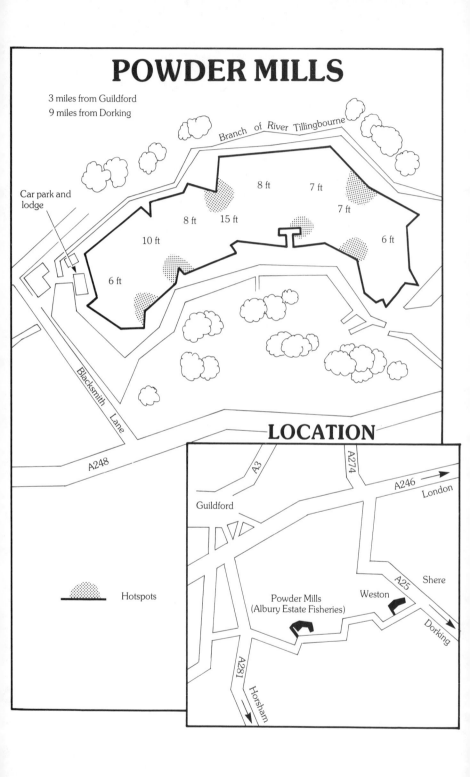

POWDER MILLS

3 miles from Guildford
9 miles from Dorking

Branch of River Tillingbourne

Car park and lodge

8 ft
7 ft
7 ft
8 ft
15 ft
10 ft
6 ft
6 ft
6 ft

Blacksmith Lane

A248

Hotspots

LOCATION

A3
A274
A246
London
Guildford
A25
Shere
Powder Mills
(Albury Estate Fisheries)
Weston
Dorking
A281
Horsham

POWDER MILLS

This fishery is one of the more recent venues to offer the small water trout fisherman top-quality sport in scenic surroundings. The emphasis at Powder Mills is not on pumping out vast quantities of jumbo size trout, but on offering the discerning fisherman a challenge. However, this venue can by no means be classified as 'easy'. The fishery is part of the Albury Estate Fisheries, a partnership of the Duke of Northumberland and Richard Melhuish, who have the intention of creating, developing and running first-class fishing in an area designated as being of outstanding natural beauty. Certainly, the fishery is tucked away in a choice valley in Chilworth, in the heart of Surrey.

The lakes are fed by the tiny Tillingbourne, once fished by G.E.M. Skues, and a chalkstream of the purest quality. It eventually runs into the Wey, and thereafter the majestic Thames, but the quality of the water is such that much of it is extracted further downstream for drinking. This fact alone means that a very careful watch is kept on the quality, both for human consumption, and for trout fishing. Of several waters on the Estate grounds, Powder Mills is the oldest. This part of the Tillingbourne valley was used for both the production of gunpowder and paper, the first giving the fishery its name. The Tillingbourne stream bounds the lake on either side, feeding the lake at the top end via a header pond. This was used as part of the mill-race system, and some of the old stone grinding wheels are still to be seen.

The main lake is some three and a half acres, and was excavated and enlarged by Richard Melhuish with the fly fisherman in mind. He used the flow from the small waterfalls at the top end, and is currently engaged on clearing much of the stream to provide further fishing space. There is also about 800–900 yards of fishing on the Tillingbourne.

Richard has his own digging equipment and has dug many famous trout lakes and stock ponds. Powder Mills took a long time to clear, as there was a great deal of alluvial silt. This meant that the soil changed continuously from sand to silt, but at a depth of 12 ft they found a tree stump that had definitely been cut by an axe! The whole area where the road now runs was once a dam, and it took Richard three years to remove all this topsoil.

The reason why Powder Mills is considered a challenging fishery is the Tillingbourne itself. This little stream teems with life, and as it feeds the lake the trout have a plentiful supply of natural food. The water of the lake is deep, running to 15 ft, but some areas close to the bank are about 6 ft. One of the advantages of this fishery is that it offers, for the same day-ticket price, the option of river or lake fishing. This makes a pleasant change, as day-ticket stream fishing is always somewhat limited, and the chance to try your casting arm at both types of fishing must surely be beneficial to the sport. I think that many stillwater anglers will become 'hooked' on running water, as it presents so many more interesting challenges, not the least of which is mastering the art of stealth. Certainly, your catch rate will drop alarmingly if you apply the lake angler's 'throw-it-out-and-pull-it-back' approach to a river or stream. Richard stocks exclusively with browns, but with just the odd rainbow to keep them on the move.

The lake is stocked three times a week with rainbows only, and the heaviest to come out so far scaled a shade under 12 lb. Albury Estate Fisheries aim to produce their own fish soon, which will allow them to bring on very big fish at a competitive price for all the Estate waters. The site for this new trout farm is in the heart of the Albury Estate, on what were once watercress beds. Here, bore holes show a water flow of some 1½ million gallons per day, and the excavation is already under way for extensive trout stews. With the trout farm in operation, Richard hopes to be able to offer a larger percentage of double-figure fish, and to bring on some large browns for the river fishing as well.

The clarity of the water in the lake changes according to the rainfall in the valley. In normal conditions the lake will go gin-clear and allow individual stalking of fish. After rainfall, the river feeding the lake via the header pond will show a slight tinge of colour, which then transfers into the lake, reducing visibility slightly. Some locals say that this is an advantage, particularly in the hot, still days of summer when the fishing gets really difficult. A blue sky and clear water are not the best conditions in which to tackle trout. Local anglers think that the colour in the water masks your leader so that the trout sees less,and also that an injection of fresh rain-water boosts the oxygen content and makes the fish more active.

The fishing itself is still quite productive, despite its reputation for

Coulsdon angler, John Ferguson, took rainbows of 2 lb and 4 lb from Powder Mills using a Cat's Whisker on a floating line and a slow-sink braided leader.

being a water requiring perseverance. For some reason the fish will usually come at one end of the lake or the other. The middle can be quiet, so if you fail to pull into a fish at the car-park end, do not stay there all day in the hope that a fish might just chance along. Instead, go straight to the opposite end, where very often you will pick up a fish immediately. You can always fish the middle section later in the day.

The fish-per-rod average is around 2.7, and in a year Richard turns over some 10 tons of trout between the Estate's fisheries. Once he starts to buy in the 3-in fingerlings and feed them on in the new trout farm, he hopes to surpass this figure, but without passing on a considerable cost to the trout angler.

Mark Carter from Purley shows off a nice trout taken on a
Pearl Fry and intermediate line.

SEASONAL TACTICS

Spring

The season opens in the middle of March and runs into November.
Basically, the lake produces best to a floating line, with the angler
trying to match the insect life with a near imitation. For traditionalists,
this water may be just right. There are very good buzzer hatches,
especially late in the evening. Since the water is set in a secluded
valley, the terrestrials make a strong appearance. The use of long
leaders, with a recommended limit of about 6 lb, ensures that big
trout can always be seduced. At the end of May the mayfly hatch
begins in earnest. There is an extended season of the most famous fly
life of all, since the river and lake have different hatching times, the

two overlapping to provide the best of nymph and surface fishing from the end of May, possibly into early July.

Summer

Stay with the floating line, and go through all your dry flies and nymphs in an effort to match the hatch. If another angler lands a trout, and if he has not spooned a fish that day, ask him if you can do so. That way you can at least determine the size and colour of the trout's feed. The lake's extensive insect life means that you need to constantly change patterns until you find the right one, which certainly makes for interesting fishing.

Autumn

The water holds an unusually high population of gudgeon, and there are no prizes for guessing what the trout will be feeding on. Add to this the population of minnows and sticklebacks and you will realize that small lures should work very well. At this time of year the larger nymphs also work: Gold Ribbed Hare's Ear, Montana, Green Beast, and so on, all fished on a floating or slow-sink line. Vary your retrieve until you get a take, and with clear, deep water close to your feet, never lift off the fly for another cast until you see it at the end of the leader. Very often a rainbow will take at the last moment.

There can also be some algal bloom during warm, late summers, so expect the best of the fishing in the last hour or so. Very often the middle of the day is slower. Winter fishing is much the same, but you can try a faster-sink line near the bottom. Fish it very slow. Owing to the abundance of fish fry in the margins, the takes will be 'nipping', and you may have to lift into them with a turn of the wrist. Autumn in the river can provide entertaining sport with the browns, but remember that it is all upstream nymph or dry fly only. You will need to sharpen your reflexes and do some serious leader-watching for signs of a take.

GENERAL INFORMATION

The rules at Powder Mills are standard. Fly fishing only is permitted. Droppers are not allowed, nor are tandem, double or treble hooks. Fishing starts at 8.30 AM and ends half an hour after sunset. Half-day permits run from 8.30 AM to 1 PM or 2 PM until closing time. Evening tickets are also available and allow fishing from 4.30 PM until dusk.

All fish caught are to be killed; fish must not be returned to the

Fish spotting is worthwhile, so look closely in the deep water of the margins for any cruising fish.

water. On reaching the ticket limit, the angler must stop fishing, although a second ticket may be purchased. Tickets are not transferable and rod sharing is not allowed. Accurate returns are essential if the quality of the fishing is to be maintained. Details of all fish caught should therefore be recorded, and completed return cards should be left in the box provided before departure. Nil returns are also required. An angler may bring one non-fishing friend to the fishery. The angler is responsible for ensuring that this companion remains either in the car park or close to the angler, and that he or she causes no nuisance or inconvenience to other anglers. All fishing is from the bank; no wading is allowed. No responsibility is taken for anything that may happen to the water or the trout whereby fishing becomes impossible. Fishermen and visitors enter upon the Albury Estate Fisheries entirely at their own risk. No liability attaches to the owners for any damage, injury or loss to persons or property, however caused. A Thames Water Authority rod licence must be held by anglers on any of the fisheries. Payment for a permit is considered as implying acceptance of the fishery's rules.

As regards the rules on the river, the management reserves the right to close the stream without notice for stocking, weed-cutting and other maintenance. The maximum hook size on the stream is a size 12 ordinary shank, except between 15 May and 30 June, when floating mayfly patterns may be used.

There are parking and toilet facilities, and a fishery office. Further development of the site is planned. The ticket structure of Powder Mills is as follows:

Day ticket: four-fish limit, £18.00
Half-day ticket: two-fish limit, £10.00
¾ ticket (2 PM to dusk); three-fish limit, £15.00
Season tickets are available on request.

WESTON

Part of the Albury Estate fisheries operates a further small two-lake venue called Weston. This is an interesting new fishery, set in delightful surroundings, and fishing is available on a day ticket. It has been constructed over the last couple of years on wet land at the foot of Weston Wood. Sizeable springs were discovered during the construction, and these promise to give water of outstanding clarity and quality. The two lakes are not as deep as Powder Mills, which, coupled with the water clarity, means that Canadian pondweed has gained a foothold. The larger lake is three and three quarter acres and has plenty of space behind for casting, which makes it an easier water for newcomers to the sport.

The adjacent small lake is fed with chalkstream water from the Silent Pool, half a mile away, and is ideal for dry-fly fishing. It is stocked just with brown trout, and is ideal on late summer evenings, when amazing hatches of both water-borne and terrestrial insects can occur. Up to 15 anglers can block-book either this water or Powder Mills. Weston is open from mid-March to the end of December. The largest rainbow weighed 11 lb, and the biggest brown 6 lb. There are also a few surprises in Weston's larger lake in the shape of huge browns.

Powder Mills and Weston are within easy striking distance of London, which accounts for the very high number of half-day and

Weston is part of the Albury Estate ticket system. A tiny fishery, but located near the main road for ease of access, and stocked with trout. Floating lines are best used here.

evening permits sold. Anyone able to get away from the office early in the day can drive down and be fishing in a tranquil setting in under two hours. There are three pubs close by, all serving hot and cold lunches. Tickets for both venues can be collected and paid for at the Albury Estate Office, Albury, Surrey. Telephone: (048641) 2323.

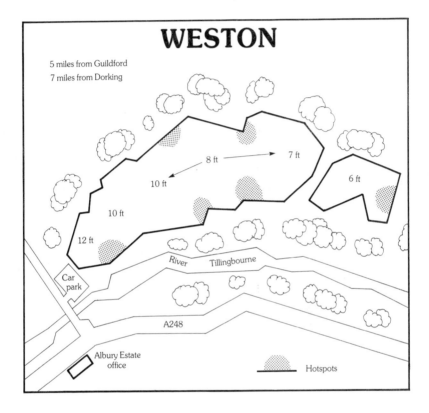

WESTON

5 miles from Guildford
7 miles from Dorking

8 ft

7 ft

6 ft

10 ft

10 ft

12 ft

River Tillingbourne

Car park

A248

Albury Estate office

Hotspots

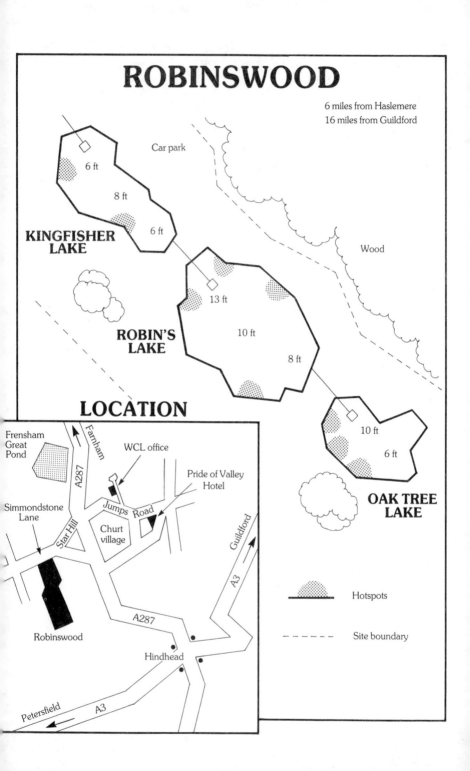

ROBINSWOOD

6 miles from Haslemere
16 miles from Guildford

Car park

Wood

KINGFISHER LAKE

6 ft

8 ft

6 ft

13 ft

10 ft

8 ft

ROBIN'S LAKE

10 ft

6 ft

OAK TREE LAKE

LOCATION

Frensham Great Pond

Farnham

WCL office

A287

Pride of Valley Hotel

Simmondstone Lane

Jumps Road

Star Hill

Churt village

Guildford

A3

Robinswood

A287

Hindhead

Petersfield

A3

Hotspots

Site boundary

ROBINSWOOD

Hampshire has a wealth of trout fisheries, but adjoining Surrey is fast becoming popular as well. This book is a guide to selected small waters, and Surrey's Robinswood Trout Fishery really does fall into that category. Although only a tiny fishery, it yields some of the biggest trout in the county. Set in a tranquil valley in some of England's finest woodlands, this miniature three-lake venue offers decidedly light-tackle fishing. I do not mean light in terms of the breaking strain of the leader tippet, as that could well be to court disaster. I mean light in terms of the rod rating and AFTM rating of fly lines. Long-distance casting is not required, but accurate casting certainly is – if you want to get the best from the water, that is.

Finding the fishery is difficult, and you will usually have to go to the main house and hatchery first, where you will be told how to get there. Located 5 miles from the Hampshire border, the lakes are to the south of the ancient town of Farnham and 4 miles north of the A3 at Hindhead. The first of the three lakes appears after a bumpy drive down a narrow lane that in springtime is garlanded with yellow, courtesy of the wild daffodils. At the end of the lane is the fishery hut, car park and the middle and top lakes. The top lake is where the feeder stream comes in, right at the neck of the valley. In fact, at first glance it appears to come straight out of the tree line! This tiny feeder stream originates in Whitmore Vale at Waggoner's Wells, some 5 miles away, a spot famous among tourists and countryside-lovers alike.

Surrounded by woodland, the first lake is not surprisingly called Oak Tree Lake. The top corner is lined by overhanging trees that have been left purposely to act as sanctuaries for trout and as a feature for the fly fisherman to cast to. So many waters are just open expanses where all you do is mindlessly throw out and pull back the fly. Here you can refine your fly placement, and perhaps learn a little about the trout's preference for cover of some kind. The gently sloping valley floor is banked up by a dam at the other end, where a monk's hatch joins the water with Robin's Lake, the largest of the

Feeding time in the Robinswood stew ponds, where thousands of good rainbows are held.

three. Sometimes, at the back end of the season in early November, it is possible to hear large browns thrashing and splashing as they try to get into Oak Tree Lake via the monk's hatch, after running up the outflow pipe!

Robin's Lake has one bank of trees, and the successful angler is the one who places his fly thoughtfully, either along the edge of the trees or bushes, or even alongside the open bank. The water drops away sharply and big rainbows will come in deceptively close. Those who are not prepared for it can be broken off, or spot the fish so close that all they see is the bow-wave as it careers away, frightened, perhaps, by a careless footfall. Then, via another monk's hatch, Robin's Lake falls away over several feet to form the smallest of the three lakes, Kingfisher Lake. This also holds some good fish, but they are wary. Success depends on keeping low, allowing the water and fish to settle before casting, and retrieving slowly.

The valley stream was dammed to create this trout fishery in 1986, so it definitely falls into the 'new water' category. Eventually the stream meanders out through the woods to run into Frensham Great Pond. Since the fishery lies between two conservation areas, there are many who visit just for the wildlife photography. The ancient woodland consists mainly of mature oaks and beech. On the hill overlooking the lakes is a badger set, which many wildlife photographers visit at night, and there are deer, too. These are sometimes seen drinking at the water's edge by early-morning anglers. There are also three kingfisher nests on the lake of that name, and one birdwatcher has a superb picture of two of these birds playing tug-of-war with a trout fry.

Robinswood is stocked from owner Richard Twite's own stock ponds, situated at the back of his house. In fact, having seen dozens of trout stews in places as far apart as Madeira and South Africa, Hampshire and Utah, I found Richard's to be the most attractively laid out. It did not surprise me to learn that he had done all the landscaping himself. To own such a house is surely every angler's dream. Stocking density is around 100 fish per acre, and any fly method is allowed on Oak Tree and Robin's Lakes, but only dry fly and nymph on Kingfisher. As mentioned above, this tiny water holds some superb fish, and there are rainbows in the stock ponds of up to 16 lb, as well as some superb browns up to, and slightly over, 10 lb. Some of the browns in Kingfisher Lake run to 9 lb, but do not come to a clumsy approach.

Owing to the abundance of the surrounding woodland, there is

An angler lifts into a fish taken on a floating line at Robinswood fishery in Surrey. A small fishery but ideally suited for the angler who wants some quiet fishing in protected surroundings.

enough terrestrial life to guarantee plenty of free-rising fish. Mayfly, sedge, buzzers – all the standard waterlife patterns will produce, as will various lures. After heavy rain, all three lakes, being stream-fed, will carry a tinge of colour. At such times it pays to try small lures, white and orange being the most productive. Once the water clears from the dropping stream, the standard dry-fly and nymph patterns and presentation can be used.

With a weekly stocking of triploid rainbows of 2–15 lb plus the bonus of those big browns, the water is popular, particularly for corporate days. These business functions are designed specifically by Richard for from 10 to 30 people, and offer both shooting and fishing. Arrival time is 10 AM, when coffee is served and a demonstration follows. Then between 10.30 and 12.30 there is a 50-bird clay shoot. Lunch is provided (three courses or à la carte) and in the afternoon from 2.30 to 5.30 there is trout fishing at the lakes, followed by tea. Richard provides all the required equipment, trophies and a brace of trout. The total cost is £65.00 per head at the time of writing. These days are very popular with many large companies, and some of Richard's valued clients are Alfred McAlpine, Costain and The Round Table.

At the house Richard offers fly-casting tuition at £15.00 per hour. You fish for trout of 2–15 lb in his clear stock lakes, using a hookless fly, so you can actually experience the excitement of a take. Richard is a member of the British Trout Association and a BFSS casting instructor. It is hoped that by late 1989 the full facilities of a clubhouse will be in operation at the lakeside, with tackle for hire, equipment for sale, and tea and coffee. As of 1988 the best bag limit weighed in at a creditable 26¾ lb, the fishery record for rainbow stood at 14½ lb, and the brown trout record was 8¾ lb. Both records could be broken by the time this book is published.

SEASONAL TACTICS

Spring

As the water area is so small, floating lines and long leaders are the order of the day. Being stream-fed, the first lake will be the coldest, so slow the retrieve right down, and lift into any fish with a gentle but sharp flick of the wrist to set the hook. Small lures will score very early on, but as the months go by the sun warms everything, and the nymphs and dry flies come into their own. A good mayfly hatch runs on through June, having started, weather permitting, at the end of May. Early summer will bring plenty of sedges, and anglers fishing in the surface film will do well to try black or orange buzzers.

Summer

The fishing is much the same as in the spring. Stay with floating lines and nymphs, waiting on until last light to capitalize on any dry-fly activity. Perhaps try a sinking line during any hot, still and bright days when the fish will have gone deep. This is certainly worth a try, and might just pick up a bonus fish or two. According to Richard, 5 PM onwards is best for the dry fly.

Autumn

This is the season to try the Daddy Longlegs, teasing those fish into taking on the surface. If the weather is warm and damp, there is every chance that they will not need much teasing, since all those trees and bushes ensure that 'daddies' are certainly not in short supply! Both small lures and the larger nymph patterns will be coming into their own at this time of year. As for lures, you can fish both Oak Tree and Robin's Lakes with patterns such as the Orange Whisky, Appetiser or a large Jersey Herd. Try a slow-sink line, varying the speed of retrieve all the time. Since the lakes are tiny, the occupants soon get used to seeing a fly retrieved at a constant rate. By speeding up or slowing down your retrieve you might just make them think they have seen something different, and provoke them into grabbing at it.

The larger nymph patterns such as Gold Ribbed Hare's Ear, Montana and an oversized Pheasant Tail will get fish, but try tying a few patterns yourself, without adding a lead underweight. This keeps the nymph up in the first foot or so of water, and again picks up the odd fish that might not otherwise have taken.

Winter

Fish as you would in the autumn. Since this is such a small venue, there are no major water changes – wind-chill factors and so on – to move the fish around. Fish it as you find it, but try white lead-headed lures, and follow Richard's tip: fish slow, and strike gently into any takes. This is when some of those bigger fish start to come out, especially in October and November before the water temperature really starts to drop.

Richard also runs competitions quite regularly, with trophies and a barbecue. Ten people or more can block-book the fishery for these events. So even if you are not in a fishing club, get a group of ten together and you can have the water all to yourself. Failing that, you could organize a shooting and fishing weekend, since these are also proving very popular. All in all, the venue offers light-tackle sport for the experienced angler and yet is also ideal for the beginner.

1990 ticket prices are:

Day ticket: £20.00 (four-fish limit).
Half-day ticket: £15.00 (three-fish limit).
Evening ticket: £12.00 (two-fish limit).
Season ticket: £400.000.

For more information contact: Richard Twite, Robinswood Trout Fishery, Robin's Wood, Churt, Surrey. Telephone: (025125) 4321.

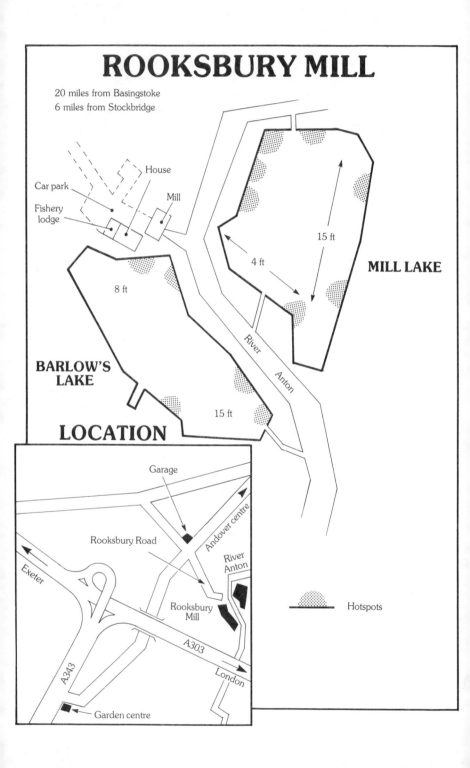

ROOKSBURY MILL

20 miles from Basingstoke
6 miles from Stockbridge

House

Car park

Mill

Fishery
lodge

15 ft

4 ft

MILL LAKE

8 ft

River Anton

BARLOW'S
LAKE

15 ft

LOCATION

Garage

Rooksbury Road

Andover centre

River
Anton

Rooksbury
Mill

Exeter

A303

London

A343

Garden centre

Hotspots

ROOKSBURY MILL

Given its location in the centre of Andover, you would think that Rooksbury Mill was just another trout venue. Yet the fishery has been landscaped to make you feel that you are in the countryside rather than close to a busy town with a by-pass running behind one of the lakes. Good fishing itself can take your mind off the noises around you until you become fully engrossed in catching fish. You need plenty of action for that to happen, and Rooksbury Mill certainly offers it. The water quality is first class and its clarity offers the chance to spot some free-swimming fish that can be cast to.

The fishery is located in mature grounds of over 16 acres and comprises two lakes totalling nine acres. There is also about a mile of bank on the Test tributary known as the River Anton. For the family who want to leave Dad to his fishing, Salisbury can be reached in less than an hour, and offers the Cathedral, walks on the banks of the Avon, and good shopping. Rooksbury Mill was originally used, in the last century, for grinding flour, and it was learnt only recently that it is mentioned in the Domesday Book. Although the building looks old, much of the brickwork has been replaced. In recent years it was owned by a Belgian who ran it as a commercial mink farm and a piggery, and also sold tyres. It was first taken over as a trout fishery about nine years ago, offering trout fishing on day and season tickets. It was then run for about five years by Pete Atkinson. If you have seen my first *Guide to Small Water Trout Fishing in the South*, you may recall that there was a section on commercial trout smoking based on an interview with Pete. He was the first manager to attempt specific landscaping at the water, clearing trees and bushes, so that an unhindered back cast is now possible.

Both the lakes, known as Barlow's and Mill Lake, were created by excavation for gravel for use in the construction of the nearby Andover by-pass. By 'nearby', I mean that it runs at the back corner of Barlow's. But you soon get used to the traffic noise, and once you see a trout rise you will fall into rapt concentration!

Pete Atkinson was only interested in running the venue as a

successful trout fishery, and set a very high standard for day-ticket trout fishing. He was very strict about the techniques he employed, stocking only best-quality fish. There are stew ponds fed by the mill stream just behind the house, and it was here that Pete used to feed on his fish with tender, loving care until they were in tip-top condition and fighting fit. In a deep pool under the mill race were some colossal natural wild browns, which Pete netted and used as brood fish, so that all the browns now stocked into the lakes are totally natural fish. I well remember seeing some of those jumbo browns, which were invariably in prime condition.

The venue has now been taken over by a company run by Nick Carbury who maintains a quality-first day- and season-ticket fishery. As a by-product of Pete Atkinson's era, there are still some coarse fish in both lakes. Some small carp were put in by Pete that now run to over 20 lb, and a couple are believed to be over 30 lb. The heaviest pike taken on rod and line weighed 26 lb, while perch to 2½ lb have been landed. Only a few days ago I fished Rooksbury and saw some beautiful perch to about 1½ lb cruising around the weed blooms in the margins.

APPROACH AND TACKLE

Mill Lake is the larger lake, at six and a half acres, and is just to the left of the car park as you drive in. There is a deep trench along the far bank that drops dramatically to 15 ft from some shallows. Before boats were allowed on this lake, the experienced angler who could throw a line far enough to reach the shelf of the ledge had a good chance of picking up the big fish ranging from 4 lb upwards. Only early in the morning would they work up into the shallows. But once disturbed by anglers or by bright sunlight, they would drop back just over the edge and patrol up and down. This lake is fed by both spring and river, and so holds pure, clear water that is ideal for supporting insect life. With clear water you occasionally get problems with weed bloom, since the light penetrates deeper than in coloured water, but the weed is now cut and removed by the water authority's new boat.

Barlow's is smaller, at two and a half acres, and has a more even depth than Mill Lake – around 10 ft. It can also suffer from weed problems in hot summers, but this is now cleared by the fisheries' own boat. Since fishing is restricted to dry fly and nymph, most anglers will be using floating lines anyway. This is a more sheltered lake, being screened all round by trees.

A smile from the author as he shows off three big Rooksbury Mill rainbows.
A slow-sink line in the large lake was their downfall.

The far bank of the main lake is a good spot for a slow-sink line, but only when there is a ripple on the surface. Big fish will take close to the bank.

Threading its way through the centre of the fishery is the tiny, gin-clear River Anton. This is stocked only with specially graded brown trout. The day-ticket policy allows for a maximum of two anglers, and advance booking is required. While a day ticket for the lakes does not allow any river fishing, a ticket for the river allows you to fish the lakes. The river, very shallow and fast, rises at Penton, about 20 miles upstream. It is full of streamer weed and you need to approach all prospective lies from downstream, to avoid spooking the fish. Starting at the downstream end of the stretch, work your way carefully upstream, casting to any fish or deeper lies you can see. Use a wide-peaked hat and polarizing sunglasses. When you reach the top of the river, take a rest, then walk down to the bottom again and work up. This allows any fish you may have disturbed the first time, to settle.

The lakes are stocked with prime rainbow and brown trout at a density of over 100 fish per acre. Stocking is undertaken daily. The fishery records at the time of writing are 12 lb 14 oz for brown trout and 15¾ lb for rainbow. The insect life is prolific, but, surprisingly for this prime chalkstream area, the mayfly hatch is small. Yet across the A303, on the downstream end of the Anton, the mayfly hatch is strong. Large numbers of mayfly have been introduced in the last two years to rectify this imbalance. There are a lot of buzzer and caenis, particularly in midsummer, and plenty of shrimp from the ponds at the head of Barlow's. There are also pond olives and hawthorns, and Black Gnat and miniature Damsels are deadly when fished on the river.

On Mill Lake you can use lures, nymphs or dry fly, dressed on a hook no larger than a No. 8 long-shank. Teams of three flies are also allowed, which can be very productive in midsummer, when you can fish buzzers in this way. The maximum hook size on Barlow's is No. 10 long-shank. In the river there are a few grayling, to which a strict catch-and-release regulation applies. Wading is not permitted, nor indeed necessary, on the river. On Mill Lake three boats are available. No drift fishing is allowed, but you can tie up to pre-anchored buoys in the centre of the lake, which can be particularly useful when the bank fishermen have pushed the margin-feeding fish out by the afternoon. However, these boats are moored over the central channel and push the bigger trout back to the margins. You can't win!

SEASONAL TACTICS

Spring

Even in a cold spring the chances are that you can take some fish by using a floating line. You may need a heavily leaded nymph to keep down a foot or so. You should also use a slow-sink line for Mill Lake, and fish about 4 ft down from the deep water on the far bank. Use some small lures as well as the larger nymphs. Two patterns worth persevering with are the Gold Ribbed Hare's Ear and the Pheasant Tail nymph. On the warmer spring days intermediate lines will be successful from the shallow banks if Damsels, and Montana and Appetiser lures are used. In late spring you can expect the hawthorn fly to come into its own.

Summer

This is the time for dry-fly fishing, and Barlow's will be the more sheltered of the lakes. Try fishing Mill Lake with a team of buzzers, but restrict movement, otherwise you will simply push the fish out of casting range. If you are boat fishing, it might pay you to put a fast-sink line into the deeps to try and provoke a response from one of those big trout. Try this in very bright, windy weather. For those who

Choice of fly depends on water temperature. Check with the bailiff first, who will be only too pleased to assist with the right choice.

like stalking their fish, there will be browns patrolling the weedbeds right under the banks, but they will be difficult to catch. Make sure you use a leader of at least 10 ft.

Autumn

Given the presence of big coarse fish, there will be plenty of fry in the margins from September onwards. This is the prime time to take a good brown trout, since they will lose some of their caution when engrossed in fry feeding. The Jersey Herd is particularly good, but almost any silver and red fry-imitating lure should produce. Never neglect the deep water when the wind is blowing into it. It may be uncomfortable to fish, but the trout will be close by, taking any free food items that drift down. If September and October are warm you can still enjoy some dry-fly action, particularly with Damsel and Daddy Longlegs.

GENERAL INFORMATION

There are full facilities at Rooksbury Mill, including a large car park, toilet, hot-drinks dispenser, lounge, rest room, weighing room and tackle shop. The shop has a wide choice of gear, including trout, sea trout and salmon rods by Bruce and Walker. There are lines, leaders, reels, nets, bags, waistcoats, hats, and a full range of other clothing, and fly-tying equipment. If you want your catch smoked, this can be arranged, with the trout smoked over oak chippings and then vacuum packed. You can collect the fish at a later date, or it can be forwarded to you. Smoking costs about £1.50 per pound of trout. Tackle hire is available for beginners or those who forget their tackle, and costs just £5.00 per day for rod, reel, line, and net. Flies and leaders can be purchased at extra cost. Tuition is £15.00 per hour, but the cost can be split among a group.

Corporate days are popular at Rooksbury, which boasts visits by the staff of Barclays Bank, Midland Bank and the John Lewis Partnership. There is a discount on club bookings of 30 or more anglers, provided the whole fishery is taken, midweek, and a barbecue or cold buffet can be arranged.

There are specific rules relating to the river, the lakes, and use of the boats, as follows:

River: dry fly and upstream nymph only. One fly only. Maximum hook size No. 12 long-shank, except during the mayfly hatch.

Rooksbury has a fully stocked shop upstairs from the fishing lodge.

Lakes: wet or dry fly by orthodox methods only (Barlow's is nymph and dry fly only). No fixed-spool reels, spinners, etc. Double hooks are not allowed, and no more than three flies may be used in a team. Landing nets must be carried. Gaffs are banned.
Boats: no drift fishing or trolling. Anglers must tie up to a mooring point before fishing, though not within 20 yards of the banks. All rubbish to be removed from boats.

Rainbow trout fishing at Rooksbury starts on 16 March and ends on 31 December. The brown trout season runs from 3 April to 31 October. Fishing times are from 8 AM to dusk. Finishing times will be posted in the booking office. All anglers must sign in and out, and all fish caught must be recorded for stocking purposes. Once the ticket limit of fish has been caught, fishing must cease unless another ticket is purchased. No wading is allowed at any time. No angler to approach closer than 15 yards to another unless invited to do so. Anglers using illegal methods will be prosecuted. A Southern Water Authority rod licence is available from the fishery, costing £3.50 for 28 days or £6.00 per season.

Ticket prices for the lakes are:

Day ticket: £20.00 (five-fish limit).
Half-day ticket (8 AM to 1 PM, or 1 PM until dusk): £14.00 (three-fish limit).
Evening ticket (4 PM until dusk): £10.00 (two-fish limit).
Season ticket: price negotiable, depending on which days are taken.

On the river, a day ticket costs £25.00 for a five-fish limit, but allows fish to be taken from the lakes as well. If river and lakes are fished, the limit is still five fish. Boat hire is £6.00 per day, £3.50 per half day.

Rooksbury Mill offers good-quality trout fishing in clear water, and a high standard of facilities. For more information contact: Rooksbury Mill, Rooksbury Road, Andover, Hampshire SP10 2LR. Telephone: Andover (0264) 52921.

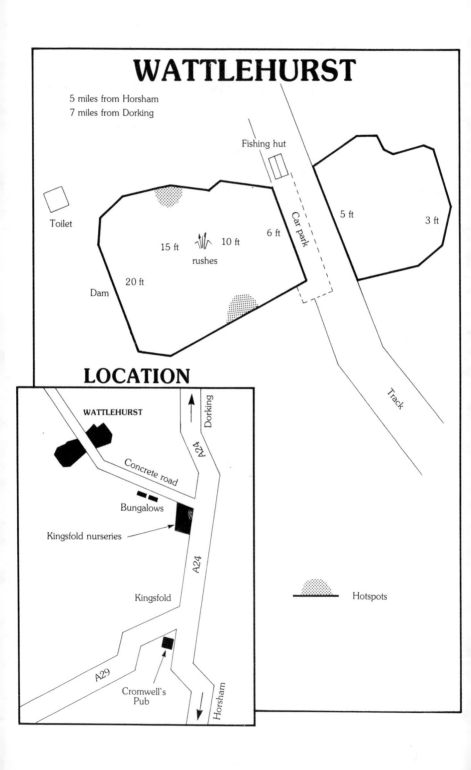

WATTLEHURST

5 miles from Horsham
7 miles from Dorking

Fishing hut

Toilet

15 ft   10 ft
rushes

6 ft

Car park

5 ft

3 ft

20 ft

Dam

Track

LOCATION

WATTLEHURST

Dorking

A24

Concrete road

Bungalows

Kingsfold nurseries

A24

Kingsfold

A29

Cromwell's
Pub

Horsham

Hotspots

WATTLEHURST

Small but productive is how I would describe the two tiny lakes that make up Wattlehurst Trout Fishery. For those who want a quiet day in an area visited by few, this water may be worth a visit. It lies close to the attractive Surrey village of Ockley, and the Surrey/Sussex border is just over the hedge from the main lake. While Dad casts a line, the rest of the family can visit Ockley, with its village green to the side of the great Roman Stane Street. Ockley church enjoys a delightful setting, and the King's Arms Inn has an unusual sign showing Nell Gwyn in the embrace of Charles II. Further south, just in Sussex, is the pretty village of Rusper, with several half-timbered and tile-hung cottages. St Mary Magdalene's Church boasts a sturdy sixteenth-century tower.

The fishery is found in a vale at the village of Kingsfold, on the main A24 Dorking to Horsham road. The landmark of the Cromwell Free House is within half a mile, and access to the fishery is via a concrete roadway down the side of the main Kingsfold Nurseries. The fishery is run by the owner, Mr Nye, who constructed it from a 'gill', which is a drop in the surrounding landscape. The immediate area was woodland, but Mr Nye cleared this, and excavated the main lake, grubbing out the shape with a 'caterpillar' and a scraper. The fishery was constructed about nine years ago, and has been a day-ticket water ever since. Many waters seem to start life by being let as a syndicated venue, but gradually change over to a day-ticket basis. At one end is a dam, and the concrete roadway divides the main lake from the small pond, both of which are well stocked.

APPROACH AND TACKLE

The lake is spring-fed along the south bank, with depths to about 20 ft. There is a slight tinge to the water, which must be due to the clay soil. However, with such open banking, this colour serves to mask the angler from the fish. The main lake has an area of one acre. Originally the water was a quarter-acre pond, and was then enlarged and landscaped until it reached its present form. The banks are clear, so you should have no trouble with your back cast.

Do not stay in the same area too long, since trout in a small pool of an acre or less soon get used to a fly line criss-crossing them. While a recently stocked fish might grab the fly straight away, a fish that has been in the lake for any length of time, or has been pricked and lost by another angler, will be 'spooky', and will move to the other end. Of course, if the fishery is busy and there are anglers at the other end as well, any spooked trout simply swim back again. On busy days you can see that the fish are much less likely to settle and feed than on weekdays, which are quieter. This difference is particularly pronounced during the winter, when, with less angling pressure on the lake, you can move freely from one end to the other.

Given the depth of water in the large lake, there are seldom any problems with weed, even in a hot summer. Both the large pool and the small pond are well stocked, since Mr Nye believes that every angler should have a good chance of a fish. He stocks, on average, every ten days, right through the winter, so there should always be trout there to catch. The average weight of stock fish is about 2 lb. No browns are put in, only rainbows. The stock are all supplied by a West Country trout farm, and are in good condition.

Being small, and with back casting so easy, the venue is ideal for the beginner. There are also three casting platforms, enabling you to fish well out in the centre. The fishery record for rainbow trout stands at 13¼ lb, and fish of over 3 lb are stocked quite regularly. One of the most popular flies is the Viva, usually fished with a floating line. The use of a floating line is common in waters that are very deep, because often the bulk of the stock fish feed in the top 3 ft or so. Deep water has two benefits, albeit more favourable to the survival of the trout than to the requirements of the trout fisherman. In winter, when the water freezes, the trout can go into the deeper areas, where the oxygen content is more stable. In the heat of summer, when any shallow water starts to de-oxygenate, the trout again have the option of going into the deeps, where as well as the oxygen content being higher, the temperatures are far less likely to fluctuate. Of all the methods of dry-fly fishing, fishing the Daddy Longlegs is best.

SEASONAL TACTICS

Spring

The water is deep, particularly at the west end of the main lake, where the temperatures are likely to be more stable. Try scraping the

Gregory Thomas took this Wattlehurst rainbow on a Montana nymph. He has landed others to 4 lb.

One in the net at Wattlehurst.

bottom and lower levels of the lake using an Airflo sinking line, with either a worm fly or a stick fly. The retrieve should be slow. If no takes occur in the first 20 minutes, change over to a small, bright traditional wet fly such as Alexandra or Butcher, and fish it back faster.

Summer

Fish the dam end still, but do not neglect the shallows near the car-park, or eastern, end. It is from here that most of the bigger fish come, in depths of 6ft or less. Fish with a floating line, but use a 9 ft leader and a heavily weighted nymph that will allow you to fish deep. Slow the retrieve. Good producers are the Pheasant Tail, Mayfly and Damsel nymphs. There is a fly size restriction, so keep to the smaller patterns. Maximum hook size is No. 10 long-shank, and the tail of the fly should not exceed the length of the hook. A single fly only is allowed, and no droppers or teams of flies are permitted.

Autumn

Slow-sink or sink-tip lines are best for late August and September, and the following patterns will all produce at one time or another: Tadpole, Zulu, PTN, GRHE, Black Pennell, Damsel, Butcher and Jersey Herd. The last-named fly is particularly good if there is a milky colour in the water as a result of overnight rain running off the clay soil.

Winter

Floating line and small Green Nymphs appear to be very successful if you fish them slowly round in a curve when there is a good ripple on the water. Try sinking lines and faster retrieves to start with, but if half an hour goes by without a pull, change over to the floating line. In very cold weather you can even retrieve at a crawl, letting the wind or any surface drift do the work for you.

GENERAL INFORMATION

The ticket prices for Wattlehurst are as follows:

Day ticket: £16.00 (four-fish limit).
Instead of a half-day ticket, Mr Nye operates a five-hour ticket with a two-fish limit (£10.00) that allows you to start at any time within the designated hours, as long as you do not exceed five hours. No season tickets are available, and the venue carries a block water authority licence. Fishing starts at 8.30 AM and goes on until dusk. You can take the fishery over for a day with a bulk booking if you are a club, or can assemble a group of friends.

For more information contact: Mr Nye, Wattlehurst Trout Fishery, Kingsfold, Horsham, Sussex. Telephone: Oakwood Hill (030679) 341.

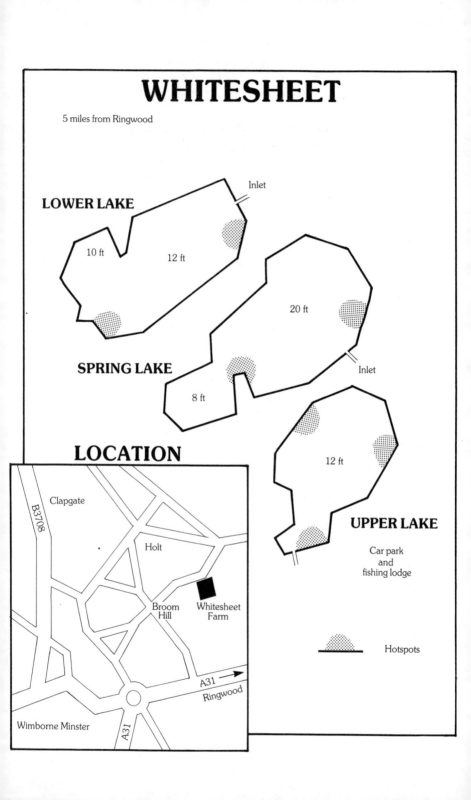

WHITESHEET

Dorset has followed Hampshire with a recent growth in the popularity of its trout fishing. While Hampshire may hold the title of King of the trout areas, there are now over 1000 fisheries in Britain where both brown and rainbow trout can be taken. Hampshire has clear water, due in the main to the filtering effect of the extensive chalk hills in which many of the feeder streams originate. Down in the south-west corner of this county these hills have a marked influence. Look on most road maps and you will see that the Hampshire Avon, England's premier freshwater river, runs close to the Dorset Stour, and that both empty out into the estuary at Christchurch.

You could be forgiven for thinking that the two rivers have equal clarity but the Avon runs through a chalk base, while the Stour rises in and runs through clay hills. This means that the Avon is clear, while the Stour is generally tainted. The Avon flows fast, the Stour more sedately. Yet once either type of river runs into a lake and settles, the water is capable of producing trout of fine quality and fighting ability. I would suggest that the Dorset area, and further west, is ripe for the construction of yet more trout stillwaters, fed by the many slow-moving streams that are the veins of the countryside. Several fisheries are already in operation and I feel sure, as the population continues to spread westwards from the London area, that more will follow.

One of Dorset's older established trout fisheries is Whitesheet. Owned and run by Phil Cook, this three-lake venue has been constructed on the side of Whitesheet Hill, giving an impressive view over the surrounding countryside. Close by are the seaside towns of Bournemouth and Poole, which can keep non-angling members of the family happy. For those not keen on the busy seaside, Wimborne Minster is only five minutes' drive away. This area is steeped in history and offers some beautiful countryside.

The lakes were constructed exclusively for trout fishing and were run as such until Phil took them over and turned them into day and season-ticket waters. The three lakes total about seven acres, and

Casting for trout on the lower lake.

have their own stock ponds. Fish are fed on by Phil, and he is currently engaged in more excavation, to make more stock ponds to 'ranch' his trout for use at the fishery. Phil was previously in the Merchant Navy, but in 1980 took the plunge into the world of fishery management.

The fishery is a little difficult to find, but well worth the effort, since the lakes are maintained to a high standard and the views are impressive. Phil hopes to have more than 13 stock ponds in operation in the future, which will mean that he can maintain a very high standard of fishing in all three lakes.

APPROACH AND TACKLE

The lakes lie terrace-style down the side of Whitesheet Hill and are fed by springs rising under the hill. The upper lake covers two and a half acres and is well established, with trees around it. The centre lake is set lower, with more open bank space for long casting on the downhill side, while the bottom lake has good casting areas around much of its perimeter. With a clay base and a pH value of 7.3, the water is slightly alkaline. This enables a prolific insect chain to establish itself, with a substantial mayfly hatch during late May and

Casting on the centre lake.

early June. The mayfly may not actually peak until the first week of June, but there are also damsel fly, loads of sedge, hawthorn, alder, buzzers and the customary shrimps and snails.

There are no islands on the lakes, and few weed problems, except during the occasional hot summer. The lakes are fairly deep, which must help to keep weed growth to a minimum. The depth in the centre of the top lake is around 12 ft, but the sides are gently shelving. There should be little or no surface weed on this lake, which is a first-class nymph water. The centre lake, known as Spring, drops to around 20 ft and is a regular, bowl-shaped depression. It is ideal for sunk-line nymph fishing. The bottom lake is shallower: about 10 ft at its deepest point. This is the favoured water for dry-fly fishing. The mayfly in particular seems to be very prolific here.

The fishery operates a rod limit so as to give everybody the option of moving around the fishery. At present it is set at 25 anglers,

Anglers fish the dam wall on the centre lake.

although if a bulk booking from either a club or company is taken, the numbers may be increased provided the entire fishery is taken over. Phil obtains his stock from the big restocking farms of Hook Springs, near Dorchester, and gets through about 2 tons of fish food each month. The bulk of his stocking is done with rainbows, and although Phil puts a lot of browns in the lakes, they have proved difficult to catch. In my view this could be due to the deep water, and perhaps an abundance of shrimps or snails. The Whitesheet record for rainbow trout presently stands at 15¼ lb, while the record for brown is 12 lb 6 oz.

While small lures can produce here, it would be fair to say that Whitesheet is best known as a nymph water.

SEASONAL TACTICS

Spring

During March and into early April, select a slow-sink line, using the countdown technique to establish the depth at which the fish are feeding. The hook-size limit is No. 10, so if you want to use small lures you may have to tie your own. The general shop-bought range of lures is available in larger sizes. Use any of the established lure patterns, although Christmas Tree, Appetiser and Viva are among the most productive. Towards the end of April the water temperature will make the fish more active, so change to a floating line and sunk leader, fishing the nymph just below the surface. The Alder and Hawthorn are both very good. There is no need for a fast retrieve. Try to stick to the steady figure-of-eight, or long, slow draws.

Summer

This is the best time for dry-fly fishing. Mayfly will be the obvious choice in early June. Sedge patterns fished in late evening are also very good. Visual stalking should come into its own during the middle of the day, when activity slows. Walk quietly around the edges, looking for cruising trout. You may be able to tempt them by dropping a weighted Damsel nymph in front of their noses. In a long, dry summer you may want to try a slow-sink line and small nymphs fished deep in the cooler layers of water.

Autumn

There are no fry to speak of in Whitesheet, so traditional lure fishing for browns is out. The dry fly will still produce, and in late August and early September try a floating line plus a long leader with either small buzzers or the Daddy Longlegs. Remember that water temperatures do not really drop until about October. The fishery is open until the end of November, so you can try experimenting with new techniques later on, but continue to fish traditional nymph patterns right through to the end of September.

GENERAL INFORMATION

The fishery opens at 8 AM and fishing stops at sunset, but not later than 9 PM in summer. It is open purely for trout fishing: there is no tackle for hire, and no flies or leaders on sale. Make sure therefore that you take everything you might require on the day. There is no instruction for beginners. The rules are basic. Fly fishing only is allowed, with wet or dry fly. Only one hook is permitted, with a maximum size of No. 10. The overall dressing length permitted is 1 in. You must stop fishing after you have reached your limit, and buy another ticket if you wish to fish on. No trout are to be returned, and catch returns must be completed to ensure adequate restocking. No dogs, radios, fires, etc., are allowed.

Purchase of a ticket implies acceptance of the fishery's rules. A Wessex Water Authority rod licence if required. All fishermen must have landing nets, and rod sharing is not allowed. Car parking is permitted only in the designated areas. At present, no competitions or matches are held here. The facilities include a car park, toilet and fishing lodge. Non-fishing guests are not allowed, nor are picnics or barbecues. The fishery is strictly for the fishing enthusiast.

Ticket prices are as follows:

Day ticket: £17.00 (four-fish limit).
Half-day ticket: £13.00 (three-fish limit).
Evening ticket: £8.50 (two-fish limit).
Season rod: £550.00.

For more information contact: Phil Cook, Whitesheet Trout Fishery, Holt, Wimborne, Dorset BH21 7DB. Telephone: (0202) 842772 or (0836) 274702.

JACK SHEPPARD

offers

Professional fly fishing tuition for trout, sea-trout
and salmon. Basic and advanced techniques taught.
Specialist in teaching children and adult beginners
to cast and fish with a fly.

Official fly fishing tutor for:

Rooksbury Mill Trout Fishery,
Avington Trout Fishery,
Alresford and
John O'Gaunt's Lakes.

TELEPHONE: Winchester (0962) 734864

AVON SPRINGS
FISHING LAKES LIMITED

Set beside the picturesque River Avon

One 2 acre lake and also a 5 acre lake

Both have an abundance of insect life, sedge and olive

These lakes are spring fed and stocked daily
with brown and rainbow trout from 2lb up to double figures.
2 acre lake dry fly only.

Also approximately 1 mile of upper chalk stream River Avon

SEASON TICKETS AVAILABLE

Day tickets £22.00 (4 fish) Half day £18.00 (3 fish)
Evening (from 4.30 pm) £12.00 (2 fish)

DONT DELAY RING TODAY (0980) 53557

ALL WATERS COVERED BY GENERAL LICENCE

WELCOME TO
DORSET SPRINGS LAKES

Situated just 3 miles from the historic town of Wimborne Minster,
we offer excellent dry and wet fly fishing, the standard
of which is hard to beat.

The lakes are stocked daily with hard fighting
quality rainbows from 1 1/2 - 15 lbs

PRICES

Full day ticket £20 (5 fish)

Half day ticket £16 (4 fish)

Evening ticket £12 (3 fish)
(4.00 pm onwards)

Fishing from 8.00 am until dusk

Dorset Springs Lakes
Poole Road
Sturminster Marshall
Nr Wimborne
Dorset   BH21 4AE

HALLIFORD MERE FLY FISHERY

Just 15 miles South West of Central London
(Open 365 days a year)

We invite sincere fly-fishers to come and try our wares in
this delightful setting, for superb hard fighting rainbows and
browns on our 15 acre lake with its islands, spits and clear waters

Full lodge facilities, car park,
toilets and refreshments are available

Group bookings and full covering upon request

Full day 8.00 am to dusk   *£18*   *4 fish*

Half day 8.00 am to 1.00 pm /   *£14*   *3 fish*
1.00 pm to dusk

Evening 4.30 pm to dusk   *£10*   *2 fish*

Catch and release - please enquire at lodge

Boat full day £8.00   *Half day / evening £5.00*

Tackle hire £5.00 per session

Credit cards welcome

Directions - 1/4 mile past Church Square, Shepperton
On right going towards Chertsey.

Chertsey Road, Shepperton, Middlesex.   Telephone: 0932 248547

ROOKSBURY MILL TROUT FISHERY

Rooksbury Road,
Andover, Hampshire

Rooksbury Mill is the trout fishery that sets the standard
that other fisheries have to try to follow.

Large tackle shop on site with everything from hooks
to hexagraph rods. Largest stock of Graham
trout flies held anywhere in Hampshire.

Fish smoking service. Tuition

Season and Flexi Tickets - Details on request

ADVANCE BOOKING IS STRONGLY ADVISED

For further information or one of our brochures please telephone:-

ANDOVER (0264) 52921